You Can Take The Girl Out of Chicago ...

Tales of My Wayward Youth

Dorothy Sinclair

iUniverse, Inc.
Bloomington

You Can Take The Girl Out of Chicago …
Tales of My Wayward Youth

iUniverse books may be ordered through booksellers or by contacting:

iUniverse
1663 Liberty Drive
Bloomington, IN 47403
www.iuniverse.com
1-800-Authors (1-800-288-4677)

ISBN: 978-1-4759-8113-1 (sc)
ISBN: 978-1-4759-8114-8 (e)

Library of Congress Control Number: 2013904294

Printed in the United States of America

iUniverse rev. date: 3/26/2013

For Florence Hoffman 1910-1963 (My "Aunt Flo")

She Keeps On Giving

Acknowledgments

First and foremost, my thanks to Donald Freed, my mentor in my theatrical life, for showing me the joys of putting it down in writing. Thanks to Aunt Flo's daughter, my beloved cousin Janet Mendel, for continuing in her mother's footsteps and for helping me restore both memories and old photos. And to my ever-present Sheldon Altfeld, whose talent, devotion and sense of humor continue to amaze me.

Author's Note

Though I have never laid claim to being superstitious or spiritual, I'll admit to a lifelong fascination with the disappearance of commonplace items—checks, letters, earrings—nothing that was simply lost but rather articles that mysteriously vanished forever from their appointed resting place. What has become of them? Clear in my memory was an incident that occurred in 1936, while I was visiting the home of my aunt and uncle on the West Side of Chicago.

Several years ago I was moved to write an account of that strange wintry Chicago evening. This became the impetus for my first story, *The Five Dollar Bill*. Though it was never published, the response from its few readers was universally positive. Most wanted to know if the money was ever recovered, many wanted to learn more about left-wing Jews living in Chicago during the depression. With this encouragement, several stories followed, detailing my experiences as a wayward girl during the mid-decades of the 20th century. Throughout all of them the recurring theme of my Aunt Flo's influence is woven. I was fortunate to have her in my life, even for too brief a time. She is pictured on the cover of this book with my brother and me when she was just twenty and had come to live in our home. This is my Aunt Flo, as I like to remember her.

Contents

PART ONE:
Chicago, Illinois

School Girl

Soon after my brother started Bryn Mawr Grammar School in South Shore Chicago, we moved just across the street to a small, comfortable apartment on Chappel Ave. where we would spend the next few years. My father's store was located on 71st. Street, a short drive (or a long walk) away, and our yellow brick synagogue was on the next block. My parents had solved the car pool problem before there was a car pool problem. Pre-schools were not yet in vogue (if they were they were certainly not geared to our income bracket). While Alvin attended school, I whiled away the hours with the usual pastimes—playing hopscotch and jumping rope, cutting and pasting paper dolls, and helping my Mom prepare the chocolate pudding and Campbell's tomato soup that was standard fare for my brother's lunch. Campbell Soups ran full-page ads in every magazine that reached our house. Each featured a different variety of soup, and in the lower right hand corner of the page was a tiny little figure known as a Campbell Kid. I meticulously cut out these little figures, saving them in a scrapbook, which I suspect triggered my lifelong passion for inane collectibles. Baseball cards were for the boys. I don't remember knowing any kids of four who were able to read, but my brother had already brought me up to speed on the alphabet. I wasn't due to enter kindergarten until the following year, and I guess you could rightly assume that I was already a bit bored and certainly not "stimulated." Shortly after the new fall semester had begun, Alvin came home with an announcement: "Teacher says if any of us have little brothers or sisters who are four and a half, they can start kindergarten now if they want."

Kindergarten? Now? Real school? Now? The thought was both exciting and daunting. My parents discussed it over dinner. Strenuous objections came from my father. "But, Mom, she won't be five for nearly six more months. She'll be in with kids way older. She's so little for her age. She'll feel out of place."

"I know, Dave, but it s just across the street and Alvin can look out for her." There was a gleam in my Mom's eyes as she already envisioned her release from bondage five afternoons a week in order to attend her Sisterhood meetings.

Pleeze, I whined, Puleeze, I have nothing to do all day! I want to go to school NOW. It was time to bring out the heavy artillery and shift into Daddy s Little Girl mode. I crawled up on my father's lap. "Puleeze, pretty pleeze with sugar on it." How could he resist? He caved.

Paper work completed, the following Monday I crossed the street with my big brother after he had finished his lunch. He held my hand as he dutifully led our way to the large room reserved for kindergarten, where he introduced me to Mrs. Majors. She remembered him from three years before. The kids were already seating themselves in a large circle on the floor, and Teacher invited me to join them. After the bell, they scurried to stand up and recite the Pledge of Allegiance before plopping back down. Mrs. Majors took her seat on a little wooden chair, and then led the class in a song, which, like the Pledge, they already had memorized. I looked around. There was not a single familiar face. Everyone, especially the boys, was way bigger than I. What was I doing here? Was it too late to go back home? Would my Mom still be there?

Starting with the girl to her left, Mrs. Majors asked us all to recite our names out loud. Half way around the circle it would be my turn. Why was I trembling? I had taken elocution lessons. I could do this. Next to me, came a voice, loud and clear: "Chuckie Samuels!" It was my turn. I opened my mouth but instead of my name, without warning, out came my lunch. Splat, splat, in a big round circle all over the floor. "Ugh," from Chuckie, as he motioned Charlene next to him to move away. Mrs. Majors took it in stride. She led me to the head of the circle, right next to her, took out a fresh, delicate white hanky and wiped my lips. The class was instructed to go on saying their names as she briskly attended to clean-up duties. Out came a steel bucket and a well-worn mop. No big deal her body language said as she swooshed up the mess. Later that afternoon, I was the one chosen to pass out the crayons. As we drew pictures of houses with chimneys and trees and puffy clouds, the afternoon passed. My first day of school would soon be history.

At 3 o' clock, Alvin appeared at the door to walk me across the street to our home.

"How'd it go, Do?"

"I frew up. Don't tell Daddy. Promise."

The Big Butter And Egg Man

I AM BARELY FIVE years old. My big brother comes home from school one afternoon and begins moving things out of the dining room, where he sleeps and does his homework. What's going on, I wonder.

"Out of my way, Do. I'm moving into the living room. Aunt Flo is going to sleep in my bed."

"How come?"

"Cause she's moving in with us, that's how come."

"I don't believe you." If this was true, why hadn't anyone told me? So I went to my Mom.

"Yes she is. But don't worry, you'll still sleep on your little cot in our room. And I don't want you to make a fuss about it!"

A fuss? Why would I make a fuss? I loved my Aunt Flo more than anything. My mother was warning me not to get in Flo's way.

"She's going to be sleeping in the dining room where Alvin used to sleep. This apartment is small and Aunt Flo has to get her rest. She gets up early and goes to work every day. Sometimes she might have company over. I don't want you to make a pest of yourself. And she'll have to share the bathroom with us."

It was the 1930's, when single girls did not live alone, even if they could afford to. My Grandma Jenny was dead, and Grandpa Jacob had just died too, so Aunt Flo was all alone.

Sometimes late at night I would hear my parents whispering about how hard my father worked to make "a go" of his Men's Wear Store. Daddy would leave the house early in the morning to open up the store and wouldn't get home until dinnertime. He liked Florence, my mother's youngest sister. She was pretty and peppy and didn't speak with a foreign accent so it was O.K. with him if she shared our home. Because she was ten years younger than my mom, Flo was more like a big sister than an Aunt. Before Flo arrived, everything in our apartment felt dark: the couch was dark blue, the woodwork was dark brown, so were the carpeted floors. My mother, with her dark hair and olive complexion and her drab printed housedresses, nearly always seemed dark and gloomy too. Now everything appeared sunny and bright and cheerful and exciting. Even my mother was in a better mood, probably because she and Flo sometimes laughed and gossiped together. Whenever I could, I would sneak into the dining room. It didn't look anything like it used to before Flo came. There is her little Victrola with her stack of records beside it. The clothes that couldn't be jammed into the hall closet are strewn everywhere. How lucky she is not to have to hang up her dresses every night. And look at this — a little table under the window with all her makeup and 1-2-3 different bottles of perfume. I know I'm not supposed to touch anything, but sometimes I twist off the tops and just take a whiff. Delicious!

During the day Flo went to work as a secretary at the Metropolitan Life Insurance Company, but most evenings she came straight home from work and we would sit in her room together. My Mom let her borrow the tall lamp from the living room. Now Flo unscrewed the bright light bulb and replaced it with a lower, softer one. Then she tossed a chiffon scarf over the top of the shade. The effect was magical. She would turn on the lamp as she removed her makeup and shared the events of the day with me. "Don't tell your Mom," she would often say, as she poked fun at some of the people in her office, or of my other aunts and uncles, especially Aunt Ida, who was "big as a house." Two decades later, as I lay on an analyst's couch, Flo's words would echo in my ears: "Don't tell your mom, don't tell your mom." Had this been the start of my mother's problem towards my relationship with her sister Florence?

Sometimes my aunt's favorite girlfriends, Kate and Ethel, would come over to practice the latest dances. They were my favorites too—Ethel with her curly reddish bobbed hair, and the beautiful Kate, who always wore her long yellow hair pulled back in a classic chignon at the nape of her neck. Often they included me, trying to teach me the Charleston or the Lindy Hop. One of their favorite songs was by Louis Armstrong and they shook their shimmies as he sang, *I want my big butter and egg man. 'Cause I m getting tired of working all day. I want somebody who wants me to play.* Although the words meant nothing to me, I loved hearing that deep, guttural sound.

One Saturday there was an unusual flurry of excitement. I soon discovered the reason, which the sisters had kept secret: Aunt Flo had an important blind date for that evening. Preparations were in full swing. The date had been set in motion by one of the ladies in my mother's Sisterhood and according to all reports, he was something special. The Date had been to college, held down a good job with a future, and seemed to want to settle down. What more was there to know? Flo had spoken to him on the telephone and said he had a very nice voice that sounded as though he was good looking. His hair, she imagined, was black and wavy and he was probably very tall. Arrangements were in place for him to pick her up at our flat, take her to dinner, and afterward, maybe even dancing! Dancing! Flo loved to dance and she sure was good at it. Now someone was going to take her to a nightclub where she could dance to real live music!

By the time Date was due to arrive, Flo looked like a dream. Her hair had been waved over one ear with a curling iron, her nails polished bright red, her stocking seams straightened, and her patent leather high heels shined. Best of all she had a new dress: light pink, with scattered bouquets of red flowers bound together by circular green stems. The dress was cut in a low V neckline, then fitted down to Flo's tiny waist. Just below the hips, it flared out into two flounces. The perfect dress for dancing. The perfect dress for Flo! I stared at her as she applied her rouge at the bathroom sink. She was a perfume-scented vision.

When I grow up, I want to be just like my Aunt Flo.

As the time approaches, my father and brother are banished way back to the kitchen. Our doorbell is ringing! My mother quickly scurries down the long hallway, placing herself where she still might be able to sneak a peek. No one thinks to restrain me when I slip behind my Aunt as she opens the heavy front door. And there, filling the doorway, absolutely *filling* it, stands a rosy-cheeked young man with a bouquet of flowers in one hand, a gold and white box of candy in the other. "Florence?" I heard him ask. After the briefest of stunned silences, The Pink Vision responded, "Won't you come in?" She opened the door to its full width as Date squeezed through the door. In the living room, Flo pointed to me, "this is my little niece." The hand holding the flowers reached down and patted my bangs. My Aunt asked if he would excuse her for just a minute and quickly retreated. I was left staring at the huge figure holding a box of candy. Striped blue suspenders peeked out of his jacket, which had come unbuttoned. His hairline began way back over a high forehead and whatever hair could be seen was thin and straight and light brown. We had nothing to say to one another. Soon I began to worry about my aunt. What could be keeping her? Where could she be? What was wrong? I fled down the hallway, where I could make out sounds coming from inside the bathroom. I cautiously pushed open the door in time to catch sight of the Vision in Pink and her sister Lil perched on the edge of the claw-foot bathtub, dabbing their eyes with great gobs of toilet paper. What terrible thing had happened? They seemed to be sobbing, unable to catch their breaths. Tears roll down their cheeks. I am suddenly terrified. What's the matter? What's wrong? It takes several seconds to realize that they are not crying, but laughing. They are laughing so hard they can't explain to me why it is they are laughing. They are laughing so hard that they are barely able to catch their breaths. Through their hiccups, I finally made out the words, "big butter and egg man." It sounded like a joke. Then they began to laugh all over again. Just a few seconds earlier I had been about to cry, but now I gave myself permission to join in the joke with a hearty, ha, ha, ha!

Flo asked me to go tell the man she would be there soon. Feeling very important, I did as I was told. It took Flo a few moments to regain her composure and reapply her mascara. When she emerged she was all sweetness and charm. The Date politely offered his arm, and off they went. He could hardly take his eyes off of her. As they went out the door he beamed as if he was the luckiest man in the world.

The Butter and Egg Man did indeed take her dining and dancing. They even had several more dates. He always brought flowers. He was nice, Flo conceded, but she soon broke it off because it wasn't fair to lead him on. Big Butter and Egg Man became a common expression around our house, one that always triggered a laugh, although I never understood exactly why. Could it refer to our own milkman, who delivered cottage cheese and eggs? I watched for him on several early mornings, but could never discover anything funny about the skinny guy in white as he quickly set down my mother's order. As for the saying, "Laugh 'til you cry"— well, I've often wondered if it originated early one evening during the 1930's in the bathroom of a flat on the South Side of Chicago.

Coming Out Even

July 31, 1932. My Aunt Flo is getting married! For more than a year she has been keeping company with Eddie, whom I already call "Uncle." Eddie often joked that he looked forward to dinner at our house just as much to see his favorite little niece as her beautiful aunt. Although I would be sorry to see my aunt leave, I was happy that Eddie and I would now be truly related.

Something called The Depression was in full bloom, so naturally the wedding would take place right in our four-room apartment. A two-layered white frosted cake was in our icebox. A little china bride and her groom stood stoically on the kitchen windowsill waiting to be placed on top. My mother had made a huge batch of her famous chopped liver. Of course, I was to be the flower girl! I would strew rose petals from a shallow basket as my Aunt followed me down our long hallway. My bangs were cut, my pink dress ironed, my patent leather Mary Janes shined. In our living room a *chupah* was set up and smiling, rotund Rabbi Teller in his big square *yarmelke* and satin *tali*t was already standing beneath it. There were more friends and relatives than chairs; they stood around the *chupah* joking and *schmoozing* as they waited for the ceremony to begin. Our dining room doubled as the official dressing room for the bridal party. I was ushered in there with Flo and my father, who would give her away. Eddie, in a grey pinstriped suit, waits underneath the *chupah*.

Time to begin! I'm more excited than Flo, who is resplendent in a new lacey beige dress that can double for the honeymoon. A violin begins to play some familiar music, and then I recognize *Here Comes the Bride*. *Dum, **Dum**, da Dum*. My Uncle Dave, who always reminded me of a wrinkled bulldog, is in charge of the bridal procession, a self-appointed wedding coordinator. After a gentle nudge on my shoulder he urges: "Now, go!" Slowly I begin my carefully rehearsed walk in time with the march: right foot forward, drop rose petal to floor, close heels, now left foot, drop another rose petal on other side, close heels, now right foot again, another petal thrown on the other side, toe, heel, toe, heel, toe, heel. Keep smiling. My timing is perfect. I don t miss a beat as I fondle the silky petals in the basket, mentally calculating the amount of time it will take to empty it. With a little luck and careful planning, the petals will last just until I reach the living room.

It was important that they come out even, that is, that they were used up just as the ceremony began, but not a moment before. My mother had impressed upon me that if I take one bite of meat, followed by one bite of potatoes, followed by another with the dreaded vegetable (which I despised), I would finish dinner with a clean plate. By the same token, I had trained myself to make the jujubes in my candy box last until just the end of the Saturday movie. It seemed important to apply the same principal to the rose petals. Halfway down the long hall, my rhythm was rudely interrupted by Uncle Dave with another tap on my shoulder. Professional smile remaining on my lips, I listened as he bent over to whisper in my left ear through cupped hand: "Save some flowers. There's going to be another wedding." Another wedding? What could he possibly mean? There was no arguing with Uncle Dave. Without breaking stride, I stole a glance down to the basket. The petals were thinning out. I had calculated the basket to be empty just as I reached the front room, but I must suddenly reassess. Instead of throwing two or three at a time, I began to dole them out more carefully. Left hand, right hand, toe, heel, toe, heel. One at a time now, and on the next step I faked a gesture, not really throwing anything at all.

I reach the *chupah*. Standing to one side is Eddie's handsome younger brother, Earl, together with his pretty, petite wife, Batya, serving as Best Man and Matron of Honor. Flo follows a few feet behind. The music stops, and Rabbi Teller begins. Eddie breaks the wine glass on my mother's living room carpet; everyone claps and kisses the bride. Before I can reach Aunt Flo, Batya and I are whisked down the hallway back into the dining room, where Daddy explains to me that, although they have already been married at City Hall, the couple now wants a really Jewish Wedding and that Rabbi Teller has agreed to perform a double ceremony. So once again the violin, once again, heel, toe, heel, toe, a petal to the left, a petal to the right. This time it is Batya following close behind, smiling and demure, like a blushing bride. I finger the role petals. They must hold out until Batya joins Earl. I can only try to make them last. Perfect! As the rabbi begins the second ceremony, the basket is empty. I had made everything come out even! When the four newlyweds kissed they included me in their embrace, hugging and kissing me for doing such a great job.

Weddings come and weddings go, but this one would never be forgotten. A few of my girl friends had already been flower girls, but not one of them had had to make their rose petals come out even for two weddings at once. Aunt Flo may have had to share her wedding day with her sister-in-law, but I had truly been the star of the show.

SAVING ELECTRICITY IN PEORIA

FLO AND EDDIE WERE having a hard time making it on Eddie s salary working in his cousin's apparel shop, so a few years after their marriage they decided to embark on a business venture. Eddie would open an upscale dress store where there was little competition —in Peoria, Illinois. It was to be called *Mr. Edward's* and it meant their moving away from Chicago for the three-hour drive. I was devastated by their departure, of course, but the blow was softened somewhat when I was allowed to visit them in their little rented house. During summer vacation my parents drove me up and left me for what was to be an extended weekend. Though I was only eight, I was comfortable enough with them to be more excited than nervous. Since their courtship, Eddie and Flo had been blessed with a very tight circle of friends, all about the same age, all married at approximately the same time. Four couples had become inseparable; rarely did they spend a Saturday night without Kate'n Jack and Ethel'n Sol and Sally'n Phil. Their departure left a big void in these lives; they couldn't wait for their first reunion.

So on that particular weekend, Kate and Jack and Ethel and Sol were all going to spend Saturday night with my aunt and uncle in Peoria. The plan was that they would drive me back to Chicago on Sunday evening.

After their late afternoon arrival they paid a visit to *Mr. Edward's* where they were duly impressed. Kate and Ethel were in their glory trying on one smart dress after another, while Flo and I helped them zip up the side plackets and adjust the huge shoulder pads. Kate chose a royal blue, Ethel a jade green. Of course, Eddie sold them at "cost" and since money was tight, they couldn't have been more delighted. After Eddie closed the store, the seven of us gathered around the kitchen table for one of my Aunt's famous spaghetti dinners. Then it was time to go out on the town to see what Peoria had to offer in the way of nightlife. Just one problem presented itself: What do we do with the kid? A sitter was out of the question as was the thought of my staying home alone. Not to worry. I could tag along with them. I'd probably fall asleep in the car anyway.

Around 9 or 10 P.M. everyone squeezed into the little Chevy—three in front, three in back. I made up the fourth in the rear seat, snuggled in between Kate and Jack. Sure I was sleepy, but I stared out of the window, intent on not missing a thing. Eddie drove around town for a while, then shifted the car to a low gear and began slowly cruising some dark streets in a mysterious section of the town. Voices in the car grew softer. Up one street and down the next we crawled. I became aware that in almost every house, a lady sat looking out the window. Of equal interest was the fact that a red light burned in every home.

"Why are all those ladies sitting alone in their window?" I wanted to know. Uncle Jack came up with the answer: "It's because all of their husbands have gone off to war and they are lonely and waiting for them."

"But why do they all have red lights in their houses?" From the front seat, Ethel supplied the information: "It's because they are poor, and red uses up less electricity."

"Oh. So they've all changed their light bulbs and now they are saving money." With this plausible explanation, I snuggled down on Jack's shoulder and drifted off to sleep.

MY WORLD TURNED UPSIDE-DOWN

BY THE AGE OF nine I had long been privy to my Mom and Dad's hushed conversations after they assumed I was asleep in my room across the hall. For reasons not fully understood, my mother had never been able to master the art of vocal modulation so, though she was unaware of it, every syllable came through loud and clear. Sprinkled in between family gossip and the status of Daddy's business, were laments about the King of England, who was about to abdicate his throne. Lately there was talk of war, and mention of a man called Hitler. A new urgency was palpable in their tone. It shouldn't have come as such a surprise, then, when my mother made the announcement to Alvin and me: "Daddy is going away for awhile. He wants to say goodbye to his own Daddy in Russia."

What would the three of us do without my Dad? Except for sleepovers at my Aunt Flo's, I had never known what it meant to be separated from my family. My life was pretty much a routine of school, dramatic lessons, and Sunday visits to my cousins in Joliet, so the announcement that my father would be leaving for a big trip across the ocean was a real shock.

Most of my classmates and friends on the South Side of Chicago were Jewish. Many of us attended the same Sunday School. The remainder went to the large Catholic Church in our neighborhood. The words "anti-Semitism" were familiar enough, but had little to do with my own life. I rarely heard Yiddish or Russian spoken. My mother was born in Chicago, which probably was one reason my father had taken her as his wife. *English only* was the rule in my house, so determined was Daddy to integrate into America's melting pot. Recently the frenetic whisperings were less about the depression and more about "pogroms." My father understood that if he somehow did not make the journey back home at once, he might never see his father or his two younger sisters again.

The plan was for Daddy to ride the train to New York City where, after a few days of sightseeing, he would board a luxury steamship named *The Normandie*. My mother was to accompany him as far as New York, where she would wave goodbye as his ship left the pier. During those few days we were to be cared for by our Aunt Flo. Whoopee!

Mom returned exhilarated from her New York vacation, eagerly anticipating the first letter from her husband. Flo went back to her apartment with Uncle Eddie and to her job as a secretary. My mother made a heroic effort to adjust to her role of single parent, an unfamiliar one for her. On the Saturday following her return, she permitted my brother to go to a birthday party to be held at the local YMCA. It was in the pool at this "Y" that Alvin had learned to swim and now he returned home from the party with the triumphant news that he had been instructed in the art of diving. "Oh Vey" my mom said as she felt his forehead, which did indeed feel warm. "Don't tell Daddy when he gets home." Flo seconded: "Dave will kill you if he knows you let him do anything so dangerous."

Sure enough, by the next day, Alvin's nose began to run, his fever spiked, and he was kept home from school. This was not in the master plan, which included keeping both kids healthy during their father's absence. By the third day, Alvin had developed what the doctor called a full-blown sinus infection, and by the end of the week, he was admitted to the Children's Wing of the Michael Reese Hospital. My mother took up vigil at his beside twenty-four hours a day. Flo stayed with me over the weekend, but had to return to her apartment in Humboldt Park on Monday. What to do with the nine-year old who must attend school? A solution appeared in the form of neighbor-friends, the Romaines, who lived close enough for me to walk to school and who had a girl in high school and a boy close to my own age. I could share a bedroom with Dolores, who had long wavy red hair and was already going out with boys. I knew the family only slightly; I had not been in their apartment more than once or twice. Aunt Flo helped me pack a few clothes in a little red suitcase. She held my hand as we walked the two blocks to my strange new living quarters. On the way over I was seized with an attack of nausea that I had not experienced since my first day at kindergarten. Overnight, the world as I knew it had been turned upside down. Flo left me with kisses and assurances that Alvin was going to get better soon and that I would be O.K. with this nice family. The Romaines were just finishing supper, but I begged to be allowed to go straight to bed. Shivering, I huddled under the blankets in one of the twin beds in Dolores's room. When I heard her come in later that night, I shut my eyes tight, pretending to be asleep. Dolores came to sit on the side of my bed. She stroked my head as she whispered, "Are you awake? Dotty, It's me—Dolores... Del...Remember? Are you all right? Do you want anything?" Instead of answering, I broke out in a huge sob. Once the floodgates were opened, tears came pouring out uncontrollably. I was so embarrassed I was such a big girl, so grown up why was I breaking down like this? Relief in being able to spill it all out trumped embarrassment. When I finally spoke, the words came out in hiccups: "Oh, Del, my brother's sick my Mom isn't home, and my father is far, far away. I'm afraid he might never come back." Left unspoken was the suspicion that I would never see my own bedroom again. I was abandoned.

The week dragged on and still my Mom couldn't come home. Flo went down to the Michael Reese Hospital to be with her sister whenever she was able to get away and I was stuck at the Romaine's. I didn't like the tuna casserole and broccoli Mrs. Romaine cooked for dinner, I didn't like studying in Del's room, and I was running out of clean underpants.

They're home! Alvin is better. and everything in my room is just as I had left it. My dog Spotty was delivered from his boarding place and ran to lick my face. Though I was back where I belonged, without my father something was sorely missing. This was taking way too long. Al had to stay home from school until he was completely well so my mother fussed over him, paying him so much attention there was none left over for me. We had to cancel my Saturday Dramatic Art lesson: how could she leave him alone? Sometimes I wondered if she even knew I was there. I ached for my Daddy's return. As the date grew closer, I began to focus on the question of what presents he would bring me. After he had seen his family, he was to travel to Paris, and then to London, where he would board the big ship that was to bring him back. Would I get something from Paris, or from London? Maybe from both.

The day arrived. Happy as I was to see my father, the first words out of my greedy, needy little mouth were, "What did you bring me?" He must have anticipated the question, because three packages with my name were placed on the very top of his suitcase. I tore open a big box from Selfridge's Department store in London. Wrapped in tissue paper was a one-piece knit dress, very grown-up, and very British. It was brown and tan, of course, practical colors that my father always chose for me. A tiny, tiny box produced a very delicate gold bracelet held together in the center by an oval disc. Turn over the disc and engraved in Russian, were my name and the date. Daddy explained that the husband of his youngest sister who was a jeweler had made it just for me. I was never to lose it. It was so delicate, my mother cautioned that I probably never should never even wear it. Into my little velvet jewelry box it went. Last came a box from Paris, marked "fragile." Several layers of protective paper later, I unearthed a plaster of Paris statuette of an old fashioned lady with a flowing ribbon in her hair. A long bouffant skirt announced that she had lived in the past century. At her side, protecting her, was a long-nosed, aristocratic greyhound dog, a far cry from my terrier, Spotty. She was so beautiful. "Look, Mama, look what Daddy brought me from Paris! I'm going to call her *Nanette*."

"Yes, yes," came my mother's response. "What are you going to do with her? Be careful to put her someplace where she won't break! Dave, how could you bring her anything so foolish?"

But it wasn't foolish. Nanette remained on a shelf above my bed for many years. She didn't wind up or move; she couldn't talk or sing; she merely smiled at me, a constant reminder of those weeks when my world had been turned upside down.

The Five-Dollar Bill

"Puleeze, puleeze let me." Although I was eleven years old, again I found myself in the whiny mode that worked with such success on my Daddy. Now it was Aunt Flo and Uncle Eddie who were at the receiving end of my pleas.

It was 1937 and America was still suffering from The Great Depression. I was eleven, which seemed much more grown up than ten. I lived with my parents in the upper-middle class section of South Shore, Chicago. My father's business was a modest success and although I had heard furtive murmurings from my parents about people losing all of their money, although I had seen men in faded suits selling pencils and apples in front of Marshall Field's, the financial crisis was a reality apart from my life.

Aunt Flo and Uncle Eddie were not doing so well. After my Uncle went bankrupt in his women's dress shop in Peoria, they stole back to Chicago where, for a little while, they had moved in with us. All the feelings and fun I had had with Flo when she lived with us as a young girl came flooding back. It was from Flo that I learned such wisdom as "water on your face only once a day, cold cream at night" and "the dishes don't have to be done the minute dinner is finished— have a cigarette, they'll still be there in the morning." Also that it was O.K. to lend your best dress to a friend. "What can happen?" Now Flo and Eddie had the cutest baby boy that was ever born. I was bereft when they moved with little Eugene to the Westside neighborhood of Humboldt Park, which was nearly an hour's drive from our house. Eddie found a job delivering bread very early every morning, Flo went back to work in a defense plant part time, and somehow they were surviving. They formed a circle of friends, they had coffee klatches at their apartment, they went to mysterious political meetings. Sleepovers at their house were a highlight of my otherwise unexciting life. I was included in everything, even when they had company. Company was rare at my own house, since my mother never liked people "just dropping in."

So here I am, on a cold winter night, helping Flo prepare dinner. It's been a long day for Eddie. He is already in his robe and slippers. He is hungry. Little Eugene begins to wail. Flo goes to the icebox. "Oh, doggone, we're all out of milk. There's not even an inch in the bottom of the bottle. I'm going to have to get all dressed and go down to Mazin's grocery store."

The pleading begins. "Let me go. Puleeze. I know where the grocery store is. We've been there a million times. I can go alone. I'm eleven now. My coat is really warm and I've got mittens and my tam."

Flo and Eddie exchange looks. Should they give in to their little niece? It is a grey, cold, gloomy evening. Daylight is fading fast. They both understand my need to feel independent, grown-up. They relent. "O.K. Kitty, but be careful and come right back. Eddie, I'm out of change. Give Do some money for the milk." But Eddie has no change. He is down to twelve cents. Flo has spent everything she had except for a $5.00 bill in the top drawer that was to have lasted until next payday.

She scrounges in her purse. Two pennies. She looks in the top drawer. Nothing. A bottle of milk is a quarter. Little Eugene's cries become more persistent.

"It's O.K. Just give me the $5 bill and I'll bring back the change."

Looks go back and forth between my Aunt and Uncle. That's way too much money to entrust to a kid. I shoot back with one of Flo's favorite expressions: What can happen?

They give in. O.K., but come right back!

I put on my trusty dark brown woolen coat. I pull my beret down over my ears. Flo takes the $5 bill, folds it into a small square, then pulls a long sheet of toilet paper down and wraps it around the bill. She places it securely inside the right hand pocket of the coat. I'm all set!

I put on my mittens as they shut the door behind me. On the second floor I pull off one mitten and with the fingers of my right hand I feel inside my pocket to the toilet paper. Then it's carefully down the next two flights of stairs to the little tile hallway. I turn the knob, pushing open the heavy door with my elbow. Outside some kids are playing hopscotch in the fading light. A few boys are playing kick ball. I make sure not to stop. Looking both ways, I cross the street and enter the warm, brightly lit little corner grocery store. Mr. Mazin is standing behind the counter and smiles as he turns to me. "A quart of milk, please." Nonchalant, like this is an everyday occurrence. While the grocer turns for the milk, I plunge my hand into my right pocket. Empty! What's this? Where has it gone? Must be in the other pocket. No money there either. Impossible! Look again in the right! The left! The right again! "I lost my money! I had five dollars! Is it on the floor? Do you see it?" Old man Mazin can only shake his head. Does he even believe me?

My heart is pounding. My eyes are down as I cross the street, looking for the toilet paper with the bill. Look on the ground near the kickball game. Look behind the bushes. Look! Look! Look! Nothing.

I climb the three flights back to the apartment empty handed. My eyes are blurred. As I tell my Aunt and Uncle the story, tears begin to fall. Eddie takes off his robe and throws his overcoat on over his pajamas. This is not to be taken lightly. His face is grim. He takes my hand so that we can retrace my steps together. "Hey, you kids! Did you see any money drop around here?" Silence. Finally we re-enter Mr. Mazin's grocery store where he lets my Uncle have a quart of milk on credit. I am a failure. I am humiliated.

Back at home, Flo removes my woolen coat and pokes her hand way down in the right hand pocket. Yes, there is a tiny hole at the bottom. It must have fallen through there, right down into the lining. She rips open the pocket, next the lining itself. Nothing! Now she does the same to the left, her movements becoming more and more frenetic. My mittens! Perhaps somehow the money found its way into one of my mittens. No luck. I even turn my black beret inside out. Finally, we are exhausted, reconciled to the loss. Baby Eugene takes his bottle and settles down. The three of us look at each other. Flo and Eddie give me a hug.

"I'm just glad you're safe," Eddie tells me. Then Flo comes out with, "Yeah, Kiddo, but don't expect us to tip you for going to the grocery store!" They look at each other and smile and then they burst out laughing. Pretty soon I am laughing, too. "Can you just imagine what Lily would say?" This is a standing joke: we all know how stingy my mother is with money. "You mean you're not going to tell her?" They warn me not to say anything about this to either of my parents. What they don't know won't hurt them. The next morning Flo sneaks downstairs to Ida Rosenfeld's apartment on the second floor, to borrow some money until payday. I know my father would repay them the money if he knew. But no one ever speaks about the $5 bill again.

The Telephone

Long after Alexander Graham Bell but way before cell phones, every American household had a telephone—one telephone. The instrument was installed in a convenient place, where it quickly became the hub of the family. Since the common layout of every apartment or house in Chicago included a long hallway off of which sprung bedrooms and bathroom, our telephone could always be found in the center of the hall, close to my own bedroom, atop a little telephone table. After the dusting was done, the dinner in the oven, it was here that my mother would spend her leisure hours, perched on the little matching telephone bench. Because she had never learned to lower her voice, I was privy to much of the latest news of the day. Sick days when I stayed home from school were the best. My room was permeated with the odor of Vicks Vapo Rub, while my little plug-in radio kept me abreast of the latest soap operas. In between the dulcet tones of *Dr. Kildare* and *Ma Perkins*, my mother could be heard cluck-clucking over the latest achievements of her friend's daughters. "She is? She did? Marvelous! How wonderful!

She is such a smart girl. Isn't she talented?" They were talking about Muriel, or maybe about Natalie. Blah, blah, blah. Never about me. I went back to the *Soaps*.

Nearly every day there would be a telephone conversation with her younger sister, my Aunt Flo. My mother was the middle sister of three girls: Ida, who was twelve years older than she, and Florence, ten years her junior. I could always tell when it was Aunt Flo on the other end of the line because my mother's voice would take on a familiar, animated tone. Either that, or she would drop it to a whisper. Then I could be certain that she was getting some good gossip maybe about Ida or about one of their three brothers. For these calls I would strain to listen. One morning, just recuperating from a bout with the flu, I hit the jackpot: "WHAT? No! Are you sure? You're crazy! That can't be! Oh, no, Oh, no. Florence what are we going to do? How will they pay the rent? How will they eat? They're going to starve!" At the sound of such anguish in her voice, I bolted out of bed to get closer, perhaps even to comfort my mother in what appeared to be a real emergency. Turns out it was.

This was the early 'thirties, when America was in the middle of the Great Depression. In contrast to their hitherto large families, American Jews were cautioned against bringing too many children into the world. A single child became acceptable, two was the norm. Anything over that, and you were flirting with disaster. With their three boys, my Aunt Ida and Uncle Dave were already over their quota. Their youngest, Cousin Stanley, was a mere child of two. They could barely manage on Uncle Dave's meager salary. Flo's end of the conversation soon became clear.

"Lily. Get dressed! We've got to get over to Ida's! Dave just called me. He said, Florence, come quick! There's another baby!"

My mother threw on a dress and grabbed her purse. Since my temperature now registered normal, I was allowed to tag along. The sisters cried all the way to the shabby neighborhood where their disheveled overweight eldest sibling lived with her husband and three sons. My mother wrung her hands. Until then, I had never seen anyone actually wring hands. Flo commanded her to stop! Finally she pulled up her old jalopy at the curb of Aunt Ida's apartment.

At the top of the second floor staircase, in the doorway of their little apartment, stood a sheepish, perplexed Uncle Dave. He pointed to the big bed, in the center of the living room. I had never before seen Aunt Ida without her frizzy blonde hair caught up in a bun. Now it lay like Medusa's, spread out around her. Nor had I seen her in anything other than her long mu-mu-like get-up that covered her more than ample flesh. The mu-mu may have been more wrinkled than usual, and the hair even more unkempt, but on my Aunt Ida's face was her serene, good-natured, smile. At her side was a tiny, tiny bundle, wrapped in what appeared to be a diaper.

How could this happen? The two younger sisters turned to look accusingly at their brother-in-law, he who had committed a terrible sin. They turned back to their big sister. "How could this happen?" they demanded, this time of her. Uncle Dave stammered. " I was sound asleep in the middle of the night, when all of a sudden, Ida shouted, Dave! Something's happening down below. I pulled up the blankets, and out came a baby!"

At that moment, the diaper began to wiggle, and a sound came out of it— a high-pitched wailing sound. It was crying! It was a teeny baby, and it was crying!

Aunt Flo went over and picked up the bundle. She smiled and held it close. Then she sat down on a wooden chair and began to rock it. Aunt Ida held out her guilty arms and asked for her baby girl, but Flo wouldn't let go, not just yet. Right then and there she decided that this wee bundle should be given the name "Carol" after the popular movie star, Carol Lombard. Exhausted, Aunt Ida fell asleep. Flo just sat there holding on to the baby for what seemed like forever, while my mother went about the business of putting in some necessary infant supplies. The new parents proclaimed innocence of any knowledge of a new baby on the way, even as we left to return home. That was their story, and as far as I know, they stuck to it until long after Carol had babies of her own.

PART TWO:
Madison, Wisconsin -
St. Louis, Missouri

CHOPSTICKS

THE CLASS WAS HUGE, packed with students eager and intrigued by a subject only recently added to the curriculum: Psychology 101. It was the beginning of my sophomore year at the University of Wisconsin. I hadn't even realized there were lecture halls this large. With dreary freshman requirements out of the way, I could now focus on the good, sexy stuff like obsession and compulsion and incest and dreams. But whoa! Just a minute here— this wasn't anything like I had anticipated. Psych. 101A turned out to be little more than a series of longwinded lectures on the anatomy of the brain and other scientific stuff. Tough, complicated stuff. I don't think I'd have gotten through the course at all had I not had the good fortune to be seated next to a good looking, Ivy-League type of Junior by the name of Roland Richardson III. Roland soon proved to be not nearly as intimidating as his appearance or his name. By the second or third lecture, he leaned over in my direction, delivering a series of droll, snide remarks about the professor and the content of these dull, pedantic sessions. His dry wit delighted me. Rather than dreading Tuesdays and Thursdays at 11 a.m. I began eagerly looking forward to my banter with Rolly Richardson. Over a few cups of coffee we discovered many traits in common, not the least of which was our love of gossip. We were not above poking fun at our world-renowned professor or our classmates. We also spent considerable time weighing the pros & cons of the city from which we both hailed—Chicago. Roland had never really known anyone from the South Side before, nor had I any personal relationship with a fellow born and raised in the affluent North Shore suburb of Winnetka. He had attended prep schools, his first two years of college had been spent on the East Coast, and why he transferred to a lowly State University remained one of his well-guarded secrets.

One Tuesday, we learned that we would both be going home to Chicago for the coming weekend. On Thursday, Roland invited me to join him for dinner with his father, a corporate lawyer, and his current lady friend. I wasn't certain what a "corporate lawyer" was but it sounded intriguing. It was clearly understood that this did not in any way imply romance, rather a chance for Rolly to be with his dad without feeling like a third wheel (I don't believe the expression "beard" came into being until many years later). Not to worry about the distance between north and south side; I would be picked and returned home safely. I accepted on the spot. The time was set, my address written out. As we prepared to part company, Rolly casually mentioned, "Oh, by the way, it's Saturday night. You know we dress." "Well, of course, I'll dress, Silly. What did you think, I planned to go naked like one of our demented psychos?" "No, no, I mean we *really* dress. It's Saturday. Men in tux, women in long skirts." "Oh, sure. Of course. No problem. Long dress. No problem."

No problem? I'm leaving for home Friday night. Today is Thursday, and my long dress is my puffed-sleeved, dotted Swiss prom dress white with royal blue polka dots and matching blue sash. I wouldn't be caught dead in that thing. No problem? Even if shopping time were on my side, finances certainly weren't. My parents would never dream of wasting money on such a luxury. I went back to my dorm with the sinking thought that I might have to plead illness and cancel. Then suddenly, an inspiration! Certainly I had a long dress. It was in Chicago hanging in my "costume bag" along with my *Mary Todd Lincoln* and my *Roaring Twenties*. How could I have forgotten the clingy white long jersey I had worn when I had been cast in a mime version of *Orpheus and Eurydice* only the year before? There it was— gathered neckline with gold braid trim, skirt down to the floor. Far more sophisticated and appropriate than the dotted Swiss with puffed sleeves and billowing skirt, this slinky matte jersey would just have to do. I remembered I had even saved the matching gold sandals. On Saturday afternoon I began hair and makeup preparations. After trying on *Eurydice*, it didn't take long to realize that while it may have worked on stage it would never do for a night on the town, for it was so sheer and clingy that my panties were clearly visible underneath. A white slip from my drawer was the answer, but was it? Indeed, the slip was white, but it was also short. It fell just below my *tush*, leaving the bottom half of my body totally exposed. A formal slip would have been the answer, but even had one been available, it would have cost more that the dress itself. It was clearly time for a hissy fit. At that precise moment, my mother's younger sister, my Aunt Flo, arrived to get in on the excitement. Upon hearing my tearful dilemma, she sprung into action. She happened to be wearing a white slip under her casual dress. Off came the slip. But of course, it was a full slip complete with shoulder straps, and fell right across my derriere. "Lily, quick, get me a big pair of scissors." Snip, snip. Flo's slip instantly became a two-parter, the bottom half of which, when attached to my own, quickly converted it to a proper, formal length. "Lil, bring me some safety pins." Miraculously, my mother (never much of a seamstress) produced an unopened package of teeny gold pins. "Do, turn around. I'm going to attach this darned thing." It required several of the little pins to securely fasten the two garments together. When she was finished, with an expression of pride, Flo helped me into the Grecian gown which, due to the sheer fabric, showed a series of little

35

bumps somewhere south of my *tush*. "No matter," Flo assured. "Throw your light blue spring coat over your shoulders like a cape. You look so pretty, they'll never notice." No time to quibble. The doorbell rang. I descended our two flights of stairs into what turned out to be a waiting black limousine.

Rolly opened the door for me. Up front, wearing a little peaked cap, sat a chauffeur. In the rear was silver-haired debonair Roland Richardson Sr. Beside him snuggled a platinum blonde woman wearing what appeared to be an ermine jacket thrown casually over her shoulders. Her intoxicating scent permeated the entire car. Rolly and I were relegated to little "jump seats" in front of his father and the blonde (introduced only as "Faye.") On the drive to the Near North Side, I learned that we were to dine at the famed *Don the Beachcomber*, an exotic Asian restaurant that I had longed to visit. It was something all right. As we crossed a little footbridge brightened by tiki-torches leading to the entrance, the *maître-d* immediately sprang into action. "Good evening, Mr. Richardson. Madame. Wonderful to see you again." Faye handed him her fur wrap and there was nothing to do but allow him to take my powder blue spring coat to the cloakroom. As we were led across the sumptuous dining room with its exotic foliage and waterfalls I was certain that all eyes were not on me, but rather a row of puffy little bumps encircling my hips.

Once we were seated at a corner table for four, I breathed a sigh of relief. Faye and Mr. Richardson immediately began their first round of Navy Grogs. My own drink was served *sans* alcohol but it didn't matter. I was in a land of enchantment. My hosts seemed delighted with my naiveté and my enthusiasm, immediately taking over the food order. I looked down for my cutlery in vain. Nothing other than a pair of ivory chopsticks. "No, no, no, my Dear. Oriental food must only be consumed with chopsticks. One must never use fork or knife." (There had never been any objections at the Pekoe Inn, above my father's store.) Amused by my reluctance to give it a try, Rolly whispered, "Don't worry.

I'll show you how." The appetizers arrived. My hosts immediately began nip-nip-nipping at their food like natives. With some side coaching by his father and Faye, Rolly instructed me in the art of holding ivory sticks between forefinger and thumb. My clumsy attempts were good for a few hearty laughs, but they were the good-natured variety and I rather enjoyed them. Bringing the first bite successfully to my mouth was scored as a real victory. As the meal progressed, and I became more skillful, I began to savor what had to have been the most delicious food of my life, ever. No doubt aided by the rum drinks, everyone loosened up and chatted away, as though this was just an ordinary evening like any other. Even Faye managed to crack her mask-like mold into a few smiles. I think Rolly's dad was somewhat amused but approving of his son's choice of dinner companions. Rolly took me home in a taxicab, while the elders wended their way north in their limo. Despite a shaky start, I counted the evening a royal success— certainly a memorable one.

Rolly and I had a couple of lunches together at the local Chinese joint in Madison after that . Once in a while I'd get a sliver in my tongue from their rough-hewn chopsticks, but I never asked for a fork again. As for Aunt Flo, to show my appreciation for her skill with a scissors and in recognition of her talent as a designer of intimate apparel, I attempted many times to teach her how to eat with chopsticks. She never quite got the hang of it.

Sizzlin' Town

When I was young, I dreamed of New York. Not mere fantasies or longings for New York, but actual REM dreams. I would awaken suddenly to a vision of the tallest building in the world (the Empire State) looming in front of me. Or clearer still, was the tall crowned statuesque lady with her torch held high. Although I had never seen either of these icons up close and personal, I had literal dreams of them, so eager was I to visit the Big Apple. I realize how Freud would interpret these symbols, but as someone once said, "sometimes a cigar is just a cigar."

Throughout high school I had become more and more involved in theatre and increasingly determined to become a professional actress. But instead of living in the city that could turn this into a reality, I was stuck in the Midwest, in Chicago, which in those years had earned itself (or so it seemed to me) the title "Second City." Chicago always lagged a step behind in everything from education to fashion to all things cultural, particularly where it mattered most— the theatre. Eventually an improvisational comedy troupe (that was later to surpass all others) had mockingly dubbed themselves just that: "Second City." Was I to forever be banished from first place?

At sixteen I went away to the University of Wisconsin where I could immediately sense there was no status to be gained by the admission that one hailed from Chicago. The Independent House I resided in on Langdon Street in Madison was the last to be occupied, (being the farthest down the hill from campus) and was filled with a rag-tag assortment of displaced co-eds, all of whom seemed to deem it necessary to attach the name of the state when identifying their home towns. The main floor housed the mandatory Wisconsin residents : RacineWisconsin, MilwaukeeWisconsin, but the second floor boasted TulsaOklahoma and ShrevesportLoosiana then on the third came WilkesbarrePennsylvania and NashvilleTennessee. Finally, above them all, was a triangular garret room in which resided Paula, my closest friend and mentor, from St. LouisMissouri. Paula's roommate was a Junior named Marian Thurman, who proudly announced her city of origin as LongBeachLongIslandNewYork .

Since Paula had attended two East Coast Ivy League colleges prior to finding her way to a lowly state institution, she had already adopted the air of a sophisticated New Yorker. She and Marian spent hours comparing notes on poetry readings in Greenwich Village and late suppers at Sardis while I salivated with envy. Although Marian's father was in advertising and she was a brilliant student, her speech, even to my unaccustomed ear, bore the unmistakable trace of Brooklyn.

Now her parents resided in Long Beach, Long Island, New York, which Marian identified as her home. Our friendship blossomed over that first fall term and by the time Christmas break was approaching, Marian had hatched a plan to stifle my frustration. "I spoke to my parents and they would love to have you for Christmas, Dee. Tell your folks we'll meet you at the train station and you can still be back in plenty of time to spend New Year's Day in Chicago." My parents were already feeling a financial pinch in sending me to an out-of-state university. They had treated me to an escorted tour in my senior year of high school to Washington, D.C. Could I push them one step further? It was time to turn up the "Daddy's Little Girl" charm, only it didn't seem to be working. According to my father, I was too young to travel alone, I should study over vacation, he needed my help in his store during the Xmas rush, blah, blah, blah. Marian came to the rescue by appealing to her own father. Mr. Thurman himself placed a person-to-person telephone call to my Dad, assuring him that they would love to have me as a houseguest and that I would be well chaperoned. Daddy was defeated. I was but a train ticket away from my phallic dream!

The ride from Grand Central Station to Long Beach was highlighted by a glimpse of the brightly lit Empire State Building. Perhaps I was sleepy after my cramped night on a coach train, but somehow it didn't seem so overwhelming after all. My host's home on a cul-de-sac in Long Beach was a one-story affair that bore familiar traces of houses in the suburbs that I had known all my life, the main difference being that theirs was only a short distance to the Atlantic Ocean. The following day we walked to the beach, hung out with some of Marian's old chums, and helped her mom in the kitchen. Manhattan was less than an hour away on the Long Island Railroad but still beyond my reach. Though I itched and ached, I'd have to wait until we were driven in on Saturday.

At last, the Big Day, and there it was in all its glory: The Brooklyn Bridge, Greenwich Village, Fifth Avenue, and finally, Times Square, all glimpsed from the back seat of Mr. Thurman's dark blue Buick, so much more spacious and luxurious than our little Plymouth. We hustled into a theatre on 47th Street just as the curtain was going up on *Arsenic & Old Lace*. After the thrill of my first actual Broadway play, Marian's dad, the advertising exec, was treating us all to a steak dinner at the famed *Pen and Pencil Club*. The family assured me that it was a favorite gathering place of the newspaper and publicity crowd. The five of us including, Marian's younger brother, strode into the murky red and gold foyer, where Mr. Thurman shook hands with the *maître-d*. (Was that a dollar bill that slipped from his hand?) There would be a short wait for our table, which we would spend on a carved bench near the doorway. To our left was the main dining room, to our right a large, noisy, less formal bar where dinner was also being served. The place was alive with tension and energy. Waiters came and went, cutting across the foyer carrying large trays at an incredible pace that would make their Chicago counterparts appear to be moving in slow motion. Patrons met, kissed, hugged, as they were shown to their tables. I caught snatches of conversation about holiday parties and hit shows and art exhibits. Each time the door opened I shivered from cold and nervousness. It was understood, of course, that this was a steak house, and that was what we would be feasting upon. The thought was somewhat less than tantalizing, steak never having been the favorite of my dinners at home. Although my mother did not keep a kosher kitchen, she and my father still clung to the tradition of purchasing their meat from Morry's Kosher Butcher Shop. I had grown up on slices of thin, curled beef liver, an occasional stuffed veal breast, or an overcooked brisket all taken from portions of the cow that were sanctified enough for Jews. When sliced in one-inch pieces, the brisket was known in my house as a "steak." It was served with mashed potatoes and was dark brown on the outside, dark brown on the inside. Now I heard the Thurmans carrying on with glee in anticipation of their filet mignon. When I admitted my ignorance of that delicacy, they insisted that I be initiated that very evening. A waiter hurried by. Above his head was a platter on top of which rested a wooden plank that in turn held an oval metal plate, which sizzled as he hurried by— a very audible sizzle. The aroma was tantalizing. "What was that?" "That? Why, Dottie, that's why we're here— that was a filet mignon!"

My coat was checked in the cloakroom along with the others. I continued to tremble after we were seated, both from the chill air and from the prices I read on the menu. So I did what my depression-era mother would have done: I asked for just a ground round patty. But Mr.

Thurman wouldn't hear of it, ordering filets all 'round, insisting that they all be "charred on the outside, red on the inside." They arrived. I cut into the still audible piece of meat. Blood oozed over my plate. Didn't everyone know that steak needed to be cooked until it was dry? Could I do this? Following the lead of my hosts, I raised a bite to my lips, expecting a foreign, chewy morsel, experiencing instead a culinary masterpiece. Was this what was meant by the expression, "melt in your mouth?"

The New York visit was over; my train chugged its way out of Penn station, making its first local stop at 125th Street, where the landscape immediately changes hue. Here is a street corner looking much like my own. Pulling up to a stoplight is a dirty white Chevy. Kids are riding bicycles. A wave of guilt suddenly washes over me. How had Daddy gotten through the holiday rush at the store without my help making change at the cash register? And how is my brother Alvin faring during the recent return of his osteomyelitis? A stout woman boards the train and takes the seat next to me. She smiles. "Going home?" Disappointed that she hasn't t mistaken me for a Manhattan native, I answered, "Yes, I was in New York over Christmas." "Oh, did you have a good time?" I *had* had a good time, but now I realized that I was very tired, too tired to want to share any of it with this stranger.

We were crossing the plains of Pennsylvania. The soot that covered my window reminded me of my mother's constant complaint of the dirt from the stockyards near our home— stockyards, I supposed, that had spawned the beef that had managed to bypass Morry's Kosher Butcher Shop, ending instead, as a medium-rare filet mignon in New York City. To avoid more conversation, I propped up my little white pillow, leaned it against the window, and promptly fell asleep. It was pitch black outside when I awoke several hours later. It occurred to me that if we arrived on schedule, there would still be a few days to spend at home before returning to my dorm in Madison. Maybe my Dad could still use my help in the store to field all the after-Christmas returns and exchanges. I might have time to work on the overdue term paper that I had left unfinished on my desk. Maybe I'd even go to a movie with my brother, who bugged me about spending more time with him.

My father would be at Union Station to meet me in his grey Plymouth. My mother might have cooked her boiled beef flanken that would be waiting on the kitchen stove. All of a sudden I had a real yen for it. The lady next to me had not yet given up. "I've lived in New York for two years now, but I'm going back home for New Year's. I'm from Indianapolis, Indiana," she announced.

"I'm going home too," I volunteered. "I'm from Chicago, Illinois."

PAULA

THE TWIN-ENGINE PLANE BUMPED and bounced in the wind like a child's kite. Occasionally a crack of blue lightening set off a spark dangerously close to the little wing. My seat belt cut tightly into my eighteen year-old waist. Was I scared? You bet. Not so much of dying as of the possibility of being caught by my conventional Chicago parents. In 1944 ordinary people didn't travel by plane; this was my first experience. But there was nothing ordinary about this night. Here I was, a college sophomore, winging my way from Madison, Wisconsin, to St. Louis, Missouri, trying to look blasé. We had taken off in a light sprinkle, bound for a stopover in Milwaukee, and then one in Urbana. Thankfully, the route avoided Chicago where, in my paranoid state, I imagined friends of my father would have been certain to board. What was I doing on a stormy night, high in the sky, when I belonged in the cocoon of a dormitory room with a textbook and a cup of hot cocoa? It was all because of Paula.

I was sixteen when I started my freshman year at the University of Wisconsin. Wisconsin had been my second choice, right after Northwestern. I had been admitted to the prestigious theatre department at Northwestern University. I had a dorm room and a roommate assigned, but at the last minute, my parents decided it best that I travel farther away from Chicago when they realized my relationship with my high school boy friend was reaching a dangerous boiling point. Evanston was out, Madison in. Thus, being both an "out of stater" and a late registrant, I was denied the luxury of residence at a first-class dormitory. Since living on campus was mandatory, I was given a short list of leftover "independent houses" from which to choose. Langdon Manor, a three-storied gabled house was set at the very end of Langdon Street, the farthest walk to the lovely, hilly campus. Starting with the tony sorority houses set close to the Student Union, social status declined along with convenience as one descended the famed street that ran parallel to Lake Mendota. In keeping with my inferiority complex, I resigned myself to having to dwell with other second-class citizens. That is, until I met Paula.

Paula was beginning her junior year, having already been ejected from two classy Eastern colleges. The expulsions had less to do with grades than with violation of certain rules pertaining to behavior with the opposite sex. She came to Madison content not only to settle into the house at the far end of Langdon Street, but also into the least prestigious room in that house— the top floor garret— which she would be sharing with two other upper class students. The luck of the draw paired me with a bright but dull virgin freshman from the unlikely town of Wilkes-Barre, Pennsylvania. Before the first week was out, I was spending as much time as possible up under the eaves with Paula who, instinctively recognizing me as a kindred spirit, took me under her wing and quickly became my mentor, my idol.

She had arrived in Madison with a steamer trunk filled with an offbeat wardrobe designed to compliment her 5'1" frame. Most outstanding was her choice of full-length fur coats. To survive a winter in Wisconsin, a fur coat was a necessity. Standard garb for a co-ed was a bushy, unflattering raccoon, which provided both warmth and a suitable backdrop for the yellow pompoms we pinned on during football games. Only the most jaded or poverty-stricken freshman failed to get a season ticket for the University of Wisconsin stadium that winter of 1942, for to pass up the opportunity of seeing Elroy *Crazy Legs* Hirsch run the distance was unthinkable. Pompoms held no interest for Paula, whose fur of choice was Somali leopard. I don't think I had even heard of Somali leopard, much less seen it, until I became accustomed to the sight of it on Paula. The coat flared out into a triangular shape stopping just at the hem of the short dresses that so well showed off her shapely legs. Never a raving beauty (her nose was disproportionately large), she nonetheless cut an outstanding figure sashaying around campus in the impractical, striking wrap, her trade mark long red hair brushed casually over the collar, cascading down her back. She seemed to know many people around campus and many appeared to recognize her. She had come to Madison with the expectation of studying poetry with a world-renowned scholar, the already ancient Helen White. Paula's ability to recite by heart the poetry of T.S. Eliot or Marianne Moore put me in awe. But it was her humor that I found most seductive and enchanting; no matter what the scenario, Paula could turn it into a joke.

To say that Paula dominated my thinking and decisions that first semester would be a gross understatement. She urged me to give up the boy back home, who was already serving as a PFC in Kansas, and take up instead with Stan, a skinny young redhead from New York City who played a wicked jazz piano and won every jitterbug contest he ever entered. Son of Russian parents— his father a doctor, his mother a concert pianist— his sophistication was beyond anything for which South Shore Chicago had prepared me. Paula also urged me to buckle down and study so as not to flunk out. She knew a "divine" grad student, now an officer in the navy and stationed in Madison, who could tutor me in Algebra. Sitting next to him in his stunning dark blue uniform, I found it difficult to concentrate. Nonetheless, he got me through my final with an "A."

By the end of my freshman year, my delight in Paula's presence had not waned. We made plans to room together during summer school in the beautiful modern dorm facing Lake Mendota which was reserved only for Wisconsin residents during the school year. Stan had moved on to what was known as the "V-12" navy program, but Madison housed a large air force base should we ever feel inclined to date members of the service. We were assigned our room, a beauty overlooking the lake. I settled in to enjoy a summer with a light academic load, and a million uninterrupted "Paula laughs and stories." I was aware, of course, that Paula had been spending more and more weekends in St. Louis recently and it was no secret that she was carrying on a steamy relationship with a somewhat older man from her hometown, but until now I perceived it as merely another in her long string of infatuations. Alfred Landesman was an artist, a Bohemian, who moved in an entirely different circle than her high society bourgeois parents who suspected nothing of their daughter's frequent jaunts. We had no sooner unpacked, than Paula made another sudden trip down to St. Louis. She was back two nights later. My delight at her return was short-lived. She was packing again. Packing a lot.

"Dee, I'm leaving. Fred wants me to marry him and I have to do it right now. He says it's now or never. I must do this. I'm going to meet him in Hot Springs, Arkansas, where it's legal to be married right away. No exams. No papers. Nothing."

I made a grab for her suitcase, slamming it shut.

"Paula, you can't leave now! The semester just started. And your little sister is coming up for the weekend. Did you forget all about Heidi? And what about me?"

"You'll just have to cover for me, Dee. Heidi will get over it. There will never be another Fred. I've never known anyone like him and I never will again. I CAN'T RISK LOSING HIM!" The packing continued.

"Paula, please wait. Wait until the summer session is over. At least wait until the weekend is over. How can I ever do this?"

"You'll do it, I know you can handle it. As soon as Fred and I are settled in St. Louis, you'll come and visit us and you'll understand why this is what I have to do. And don't forget, Dee, he's got a younger brother already champing at the bit to meet you!" Her suitcase slammed shut.

When I met her at the Madison Union Railway Station on Saturday, Heidi burst into tears and wailed in her Missouri drawl "What ah you all sayin'? How could she? Just like Paula! What am ah goin' to tell mah parents? This is goin' to kill them!"

I showed Heidi around campus: the Student Union, the Chocolate Shoppe, Bascom Hall. She did survive the weekend and her parents both lived until well into their 'nineties. And some weeks later, in the middle of a stormy night, I found myself in a little twin-engine plane.

RUDE AWAKENING

THE RAIN HAD STOPPED by the time the DC7 touched down at the St. Louis airport, though the ground was still covered with that glistening moisture that a cinematographer would kill for. I made my way down the portable staircase, straining to see Paula. And there, as promised, was my redheaded college chum, waving and smiling as she clung to the arm of a tall, angular young man— her new husband, Alfred. We made our way to the edge of the runway where, like a scene from *Casablanca* stood a dark man leaning on a woody station wagon. A station wagon! A woody! After years of my father's light grey Plymouth sedans, a beat-up Ford wagon was a vehicle that oozed adventure. It was the car used to haul the art objects and crystal chandeliers that were part and parcel of the Landesman's thriving antique business. The worn leather seats revealed telltale signs of the active life it had led.

Introductions were quickly made. As promised, here was Jay, the youngest brother of the family, waiting to meet the college roommate of his new sister-in-law. Even in the dim light, I knew he was the most attractive man I had ever seen. Was it possible he would be remotely interested in me? We slid into the back seat, as Fred took the wheel and Paula faced front beside him, turning occasionally to beam at us. The repartee and laughs began at once. Without hesitation I launched into an account of my harrowing flight from Madison, complete with imitations of some of my fellow passengers. The laughs came at once. I had passed muster. I was a hit. (I couldn't have known it then, but I was granted almost immediate acceptance into the society that decades later became known as *Landesmania*). Without hesitation Jay leaned over and began his moves. Having been warned by Paula in advance that the brothers from St. Louis, unlike the boys from back home, would not "put up with any nonsense about waiting until the third date," I made no effort to resist. He didn't even know me, but was it possible that he already liked me — not just some amorphous college girl who had suddenly materialized but the actual "me?" It seemed too easy, too good to be true.

The ancient apartment that Jay shared with his mother bore little resemblance to those with which I was familiar. For one thing, it was absolutely huge; for another it was filled with pieces of massive furniture and bric-a-brac that had no apparent relationship to one another. Already assorted friends were drifting in and out. A large table in the dining room held snacks; on the old mahogany sideboard a well-stocked bar had been set up. (This was the night I first discovered that gin, mixed with just a little vermouth and plenty of ice was not bad tasting at all.) What lighting there was, was low, very low, adding to an air of unreality of the scene. What was most memorable, though, was the music. From a record player came an endless sound of smooth, slow jazz. Furniture had been pushed aside, creating plenty of space for a dance floor, and Jay wasted no time in taking me in his arms to possessively sway to the seductive sounds of Billie Holliday. I had always been insecure about my dancing ability, but now it was of no consequence. We were locked, absolutely locked, against each other, moving so very slightly. Jay's lean body, encased in obscenely tight pin-whale corduroy left little to the imagination. Billie crooned. *Living for you. I'm living for you, When you're in love, and I'm sooo in love, there's nothin' in life but you.* Was this to become "our" song?

It was way after midnight when Jay led me down the long hallway, past the room into which his mother had long since retired, and into the bedroom that held a big brass bed— the first I ever beheld close up. Faithful to my promise to Paula, I made no move to resist. A wise decision. After a night of endless surprises and delights, I fell into a deep, exhausted sleep, only to have it rudely interrupted by a large bang, followed by a sudden, loud knock, then the unmistakable rattling of a doorknob. "Jay!" came a high-pitched, shrill voice, "Jay! Breakfast!" Then again, this time coming from the kitchen in the front of the apartment, "Irving! Get up! Breakfast."

Irving?" (Only later did I discover that, in deference to F. Scott Fitzgerald's Gatsby, Jay had switched the order of his given name.)

"O.K., O.K. Cutie, we'll be right there!"

I swung into panic mode. Instinctively reaching down to pull the sheet around my shoulders. "Oh, God, who's that?"

"My Mother- Cutie- you met her last night. Don't you remember?"

"Your Mother? Does she know I'm here? What should we do?" Visions of my parents arriving momentarily on the doorstep were already going through my head.

"Go out and have breakfast, of course. I'm starved, aren't you?"

There was nothing to do but accept the robe Jay offered and follow him out to the imposing old kitchen where a table had been laid with steaming coffee, scrambled eggs, and toast in a sterling silver English caddy. Vertical toast. Another first.

The beaked nose, slightly cockeyed matriarch of the family, all adorable 4'11" of her, had little interest in either small talk or introductions. She vaguely remembered me from the night before and accepted me as merely another in Jay's long string of overnighters. Last thing on her mind would have been to inquire about my heritage or advise my family of their daughter's whereabouts. What was of paramount importance to her was that we finish breakfast so that she could get down to the store, where she was expecting the delivery of an estate sale.

With his mother gone, I was free to explore Jay's flat. By light of day, it appeared even more bizarre, more intimidating, the furniture even more massive. Endless gargoyles holding lampshades accusingly peered out at me. Umbrella stands and coat racks blocked easy access to the bathroom, where Jay was leisurely soaking in a claw-foot tub. His invitation to join him was prudently, somewhat sheepishly, refused.

In the bedroom I hastily retrieved an appropriate wardrobe from my overnight case, all the while studying the endless *tchotchkes* that were everywhere. An array of hatpins, cuff links, exotic coins, literally covered the marble dresser top.

When finally Jay emerged, dressed in tight black pants and white shirt, he donned a Panama hat, picked up one of his walking sticks, and prepared to show his new girl around his hometown. Was it possible that I had merely been sleepwalking for almost two decades? Would my life ever be the same? It never was.

ENGAGEMENT RING

AFTER THE FIRST WEEKEND, it was settled. I was in love. I returned to Wisconsin in a mixed state of euphoria and confusion. Could this be the "real thing"? How had this happened? Before Paula eloped with Fred, she had protested that she simply couldn't let him out of her life. Now was I to feel the same about Jay? There was a difference: I was barely over eighteen years old. I was in the middle of college. Life, with its endless possibilities, was just beginning to open. As my Aunt Flo had predicted, I had become politically active. I was intellectually stimulated. And not to be dismissed was the secret notion that I could still someday become a professional actress. Committing to Jay meant putting an end to all that, yet I must not let him go. I believed he felt the same about me.

Now began a series of secret weekend trips to St. Louis this time by train. It was necessary to cross Union Station in Chicago in order to make a connection to St. Louis. I lived in terror of being "caught" by my parents.

Those weekends were tempestuous, delectable. We never again stayed in Cutie's apartment, but moved instead to the little hideaway that Jay had made himself in the basement of the Landesman Antique Shop. Amidst overstuffed chaise lounges and alabaster cherubs that had made their way down from the cluttered gallery above, was a narrow bed, a toilet and a shower. It was heaven. In addition to being our love nest, it was quite possibly the coolest sleeping quarter in the state of Missouri. This was summer, when no city on earth can surpass St. Louis for heat and humidity. We would steal there and fall into the narrow bed after a night of heavy partying, and sleep until we heard Cutie open the store and putter around upstairs. Then it was up to the Rex Cafe for an early breakfast pastrami sandwich. Next came a series of habitual "Jay rounds" in which I was included. University Avenue was wall-to-wall antique stores and I was introduced proudly to Jay's fellow shopkeepers. Among his favorites was a white-haired, plump lady named Cunningham Walsh, who had sold antique jewelry at the same location forever. Were it not for an exotic tortoise comb that held her mane of hair in place, she might have been mistaken for the local librarian. Cutie, of course, did not hold her in high esteem, dismissing her as a "seller of trinkets." Cunningham taught me all I ever would need to know about gold bracelets and bar pins, not to mention rings.

One Saturday, after coffee, Jay made it clear to Cunningham that she was to help me select a ring that would signify our engagement. Engagement? This was it, then? A commitment? What about my degree, my acting career? Still, I couldn't bear the thought of losing Jay and began trying on one band after another, all with red or blue or green stones, some of which were worn so thin or their prongs so loose that they threatened to come apart right there in the shop. The three of us got into the spirit of things, but for some reason there was something wrong with every ring I tried on. In addition to being either too tight or too loose, none of them "felt right." Nothing really "spoke" to me. Nothing, that is, until I moved away from Cunningham's cases of sapphires and garnets, and fastened on to her section of rings set with the loveliest gems I had ever beheld. These iridescent stones were both exquisite and fascinating. They appeared alive as their multi-colored specks changed from shiny to dull, to varying pastel hues even as I looked at them. Regardless of their size, I found each one unique and interesting, far more than even diamonds, which had never held any allure for me.

"Oh, Cunningham! What are these?" At once I sensed a change in Cunningham's demeanor. Her tone became cold, severe. "Why, those are opals, Dear."

"Opals? Oh, yes. They're beautiful! Let me try this one on. And that one, and the one at the end, please! I love them!"

Was it my imagination, or did Ms. Walsh and my lover exchange furtive glances? One after another I put the rings on the third finger of my left hand. Some had one large oval in the center, others held two or three rows of smaller stones curving around rococo gold bands. I was a kid in a candy store.

"Why not try this topaz, Dear? Or that amber? So good with your coloring."

Jay now stood to one side, suddenly disinterested in the whole venture. He appeared to be sidling towards the front door.

I plowed on, smitten by a lovely single round opal surrounded by burnished gold that miraculously fit perfectly. I held up my left hand.

From Cunningham: "I can't sell you that ring, Jay. Opals are bad luck! Surely you know that?"

And with that, she did an about-face and repaired to the rear of her shop.

"Oh, Jay, that's just superstition! Can't I have this ring?"

"Sorry, Dee. No sale. Come on, let's get out of here."

The magic moment having passed, off we went to an auction of porcelain figurines.

The Show Must Go On

By the following summer I had become less certain that Jay was my destiny. Never fond of travel, he had insisted that our rendezvous all take place only on his own turf, his comfort zone — St. Louis. The one time he visited me in Madison there was a "fish out of water" feel rendering him incapable of relaxing or enjoying the impressive college town. Our one visit to Chicago, where he had dinner at the home of my parents was, of course, was an unmitigated disaster. It did, however, provide plenty of comic material for the Landesman brothers for years to come. My mother and father, totally on another planet, eyed him suspiciously, bewildered at his strange wardrobe and even stranger sense of humor. This would never do as husband material!

As the spring semester wound down, I sensed that it might be the right time for me to take a break from our romance and to get a little life experience under my belt. Now seemed the appropriate time to test the waters as an actress. The East Coast was a must, of course. Accordingly, I took a job as an apprentice in a summer stock company in Great Neck,

New York, headed by the famed German Brechtian director, Erwin Piscator. The summer season was the perfect place to experience the grind of continually changing shows, and possibly changing men as well. I left for Great Neck not only with Jay's approval, but his blessings, or so I thought. It would be a good talking point to brag to his artist and writer friends in St. Louis that his girlfriend was trotting the boards in New York. By summer's end perhaps our commitment would only grow stronger. Perhaps I would even accept a ring and a date.

The summer schedule consisted of six plays in eight weeks, and even with three different directors sharing the chores, the pace was mind-boggling. Good fortune smiled on me in the form of Claire Booth Luce's popular play, *The Women*. With the dearth of male actors, it was a perfect choice. There were roles for all the women of the company. I was given the part of the manicurist in Act I. Tiny though the role might be, it was pivotal and consisted of a monologue that is a real showstopper. The round of applause each evening at the end of my scene put me on cloud nine. At the final curtain I shared applause with our Leading Lady, Elaine Stritch, who had recently arrived from Michigan and was now Broadway- bound for the start of a stupendous career.

Between rehearsals I began an affair with the company's only resident leading man. Robert, scion of a famed theatrical family, was for better or worse, classified 4F —unfit for service. This meant he was free to spend the entire summer at Great Neck polishing his so-called craft. Though he loved the process of acting, he loved Irish whiskey even more. Like Jay, he was handsome, dark, interesting, exotic. The similarities stopped there, but that was enough for me to volunteer to help him with his lines. Robert was to play the role of a young Welsh miner in the upcoming production of Emlyn William's groundbreaking play, *The Corn is Green*. He was a natural for the role of Morgan Evans. If only he was able to memorize all that dialogue before the opening! We began our cueing sessions at the little tavern next to the theatre. At closing time, it was a natural progression to Bob's furnished room upstairs in a house nearby and once there, into his bed. What followed was weeks of lusty sex without the baggage of commitment or remorse. Often it seemed futile to bother returning to my own quarters. Slightly hung over, the next morning I would tiptoe up to my room for a change of clothes before dashing to my early class in diction or fencing. My roommate, a theatre major at Yale, was so determined to wring out every ounce of experience from her summer, that she scarcely noticed my absence. (Not surprisingly, she became a hot Broadway director not too many years later.)

Though I heard little from Jay, I was confident that we would reunite. I would route my Chicago train ticket via St. Louis, where Jay would meet me at the station, possibly with a ring from Cunningham Walsh's jewelry shop. I would not object if it were to be set with a tasteful diamond. During my triumphant run as the manicurist, I invited Gertie, Jay's only sister, to come to a performance. It was a short trip from her home in Stamford, Connecticut, and we managed to squeeze in a brief dinner before the curtain. Although we had met only a few times, there was a warm bond between us. My assumption was that Gert assumed that one day we would be part of the same family. Vague rumblings, via Paula, had reached me that Jay was going around with a girl named Pat. "So," I ventured during dinner, "what's going on with Jay? What's with this other woman?"

Gertie dismissed it lightly, "Oh, yeah, he's dating this waitress, or hairdresser, or something. Not to worry. He would never get serious about her." I filed this in the back of my mind and accepted Gert's warm embrace after the show.

Meanwhile, *The Corn is Green* was getting ready to open, with an outstanding German actress (mistress of the director) in the lead. Robert had better shape up. After the opening, he was able to relax regarding his lines, but the pressure to make his entrance on time grew greater. Each evening about an hour before curtain he could be found at his favorite perch in the watering hole next door. Already in costume and makeup, he would delay his departure until the last minute, cutting it closer and closer. Since it was only a few yards from the bar to the backstage door, if timed perfectly he could coordinate his appearance in the opening act. While there was a general concern among the company, and particularly the stage manager, as to his whereabouts, a certain little apprentice was able to calm their fears. "Don't worry. I'll get him." A quick dash next door, a gentle nudge. "Come on, Robert. It's a full house. Almost time for your entrance!" He always made it in time. Just in time.

After my mini-triumph in *The Women* the director had enough faith in me to assign me as the understudy to Bessie Watty, the marvelous ingénue role in *Corn is Green*. Never afforded the luxury of a rehearsal, I compulsively followed the Broadway actress' every move from the wings, lest I actually be called upon to replace her. In addition, I was to be one of the walk-on townspeople. Between making certain Robert never missed his cue, studying Virginia's performance, getting into my own costume and makeup, I had my hands full.

The run was nearly over; the last performance about to begin, when, as I emerged from the dressing room, I heard the stage manager shout my name. "Telephone call for you. But hurry! I'm about to call places."

Telephone call for me? Backstage? Who even knew this number? Immediately my mind shot to the bartender next door. Was Robert still there, too plastered to make it on his own for his entrance? The earpiece dangled from the wall phone near the stage door.

"Hello? Yes, this is her...she"

"Western Union calling. I have telegram for you."

Before the war, boys in brown uniforms on two-wheel bicycles delivered telegrams. You would be handed a yellow teletyped message in a thin envelope, you signed for it, tipped the boy, and were free to keep a copy of that bit of urgent news or note of congratulations forever. But this was wartime when those young Western Union messengers were serving overseas making our country safe for Democracy. Now the telephone was the standard means of communication.

An anonymous monotone delivered the copy.

"Ready? Married today. Stop. O.K. Stop. Love. Stop. Signed, Jay. Do you want me to repeat that?"

The receiver froze in my hand, along with the moment in time. "No, no. that won't be necessary."

I replaced the receiver just in time to hear "Places!"

In a daze I heard my cue and made my entrance. What was that old saying? Something about "The Show Must Go On?"

ᴮREAKING ᴛHE ᴿULES

I ʀᴇᴘʟᴀᴄᴇᴅ ᴛʜᴇ ʀᴇᴄᴇɪᴠᴇʀ in its cradle on the wall phone. Weak knees, pounding heart, I couldn't move. The stage manager's call came loud and clear: "Places! Places everyone!" Now it was Bob Carricart's turn to shove me on stage just in time to make my entrance on cue. I walked through my bit role in *The Corn is Green* on automatic pilot, but my mind was spinning. Jay was married. Was this bad news or good news? It could only be for the good. Of course, I was crushed. Of course my ego was bruised. On the other hand, perhaps now I could move on with my life. Deep down inside I had always known that my future would not be with Jay. He was not the right man for me. So he was married. So it was over. So good. Finish the summer season in Great Neck. Return to school. Get my degree. Enter the real world. *Finito*, Jay. This could only be a good thing.

Now a change of plans had to be implemented. Now I could no longer consider routing my Southern Pacific Railway ticket through St. Louis. Instead, I would spend the few weeks before starting my junior year at the University of Wisconsin at my parent's home in Chicago. I commiserated with Paula. Somewhat guilt-ridden over keeping the intensity of Jay's romance hidden from me, she protested vehemently when I sadly confided that our visits must come to an end. "Don't be ridiculous, Dee. You'll stay here with Fred and me. We've got scads of room. And there are loads of interesting men around. Make sure you get here by the 26th. Jay and Pat are having a big party and you're invited." Oh, no. I protested. I couldn't. Couldn't face it. Or could I? Wasn't this part of the "getting on with my life?"

I was an outsider at the final cast party in Great Neck. After all, I wasn't truly a part of this company, many of whom would go on working together in New York City. My relationship with Robert Carricart had reached its inevitable conclusion. By mutual unspoken consent, we agreed that our summer fling was no more than that. I headed to Greenwich Village to spend a couple of days with my friend Tashka who was working in a bookshop. She was already immersed in the rhythm that was Greenwich Village, partying with poets and artists, drinking and talking late into the night at the Cedar Tavern. Again, I was the outsider. Too young, too naive, in over my head. Only in St Louis had I felt a sense of belonging. Now I had ruined that with the foolish mistake of running off to Great Neck for the summer instead of protecting my precious relationship with Jay.

I telephoned my Aunt Flo. It was our custom that Aunt Flo was the one who drove downtown to meet me at the railway station. If I was to come in via St. Louis instead of New York, I'd have to let her know. I tried to sound light-hearted and casual. No big deal. Just spending a few days with my old college chum. She sensed I wasn't really leveling with her, but agreed to meet me whenever I arrived. "Have a good time, Kiddo. We miss you. I can't wait to see you." I hung up the phone. Hearing Flo's voice gave me permission to do what I wanted to do since that fatal phone call — I cried. Tears came woefully, wonderfully, until at last there were no more. I blew my nose, dried my bloodshot eyes, and prepared to move forward.

The club car was filled with G.I's on furlough. A smile from a PFC across the aisle did nothing to relieve my apprehension. My usual Canadian Club and ginger ale failed to lift my spirits. There was still a nagging feeling that I was not doing the right thing by returning to St. Louis while the bruise was so raw. On the other hand how could I resist the temptation of going back?

The sense of excitement as I *schlepped* my heavy suitcase down the three steep steps of the coach was again replaced by anxiety—that is, until I spotted Paula and Fred and their new baby, Rocco. The laughs began at once. On the drive to their house they needed to hear everything about my summer stock experience, and I soon found my old rhythm as comedienne/raconteur returning.

In my absence, Paula and Fred had bought an old mansion on Westminister Place, just behind the antique shop. Their wide, tree-lined street had once been home to the elite of St. Louis. Now it reeked "faded gentility" but the house was spacious and warm boasting a fireplace in nearly every room, including the boudoir assigned to me. I would have been content to remain there forever. After the grand tour of the house, it was time to start preparations for the big event that night. My anxiety as I tried on one outfit after another soon accelerated into what could only be compared to a severe case of stage fright. By evening curiosity had overcome fear. I longed to see Jay again and even more, I needed to see my replacement. After trying and discarding several potential outfits, I finally settled on what was even then known as a "basic little black dress." An antique gold bracelet, a gift from Jay, was my sole jewelry.

As we mounted the steep flight of steps to what appeared to be a large loft, music and voices floated down. Though I had expected a party, I was totally unprepared for the noise level or the sight that greeted me.

The evening was already in full swing. The two busiest areas were the bar and the bed. Dominating the room was a massive, truly massive, monstrosity that had been acquired by Jay and Pat at auction. There could not have been too many opposing bids for this piece of fantasy furniture, complete with dwarfs on four-posters balancing a canopy. Large enough to sleep six, it was of course a major conversation piece and the pride and joy of the newlyweds. Now I saw it only as the place on which reposed Himself, the love of my life, looking more outrageous and sexier than I could have believed. My knees were shaking as I caught a glimpse of him entertaining a throng on the huge mattress. Out of the corner of his eye, he saw me enter with Paula and was on his feet in a split second. His first act after an initial peck on my cheek was to look around for Pat, in order to introduce us. "O.K." I thought, "let's just get this over with."

If Pat viewed me as any sort of threat, she was certainly good at concealing it. A tall young woman, you might have passed her on the street without a second glance. With a toss of her dishwater blonde hair, she acknowledged me casually before setting off on her rounds as hostess. Jay put a drink in my hand and steered me to the bed, where I was invited to join in the heated conversation already in progress. Could these people all be from St. Louis? It felt more like New York and rightly so, because two of Jay's visiting poet friends from The Village, ensconced on the communal mattress, seemed right at home. One was the familiar Clellon Holmes, the other a weird looking guy by the strange name of Kerouac. By far the star of the evening was a Missouri playwright whose play, *Come Back, Little Sheba*, would soon win a Pulitzer Prize. With his quiet, unassuming air, William Inge seemed somewhat out of place and wary at what he sensed might be adulation. I liked him at once. He put me at ease, seeming to empathize as my eyes roamed the room, unable to allow Jay out of my line of vision.

A little dancing, a lot of drinking, the party continued until late into the night. Finally, the crowd began to thin and I caught sight of Paula and Fred bidding their good nights, preparing to leave. When I made my move to join them, Jay intruded, insisting that I would be seen safely home. It had been a long day. I was exhausted and would have been happy to escape to the privacy of my guest room on Westminister Place. Instead, one more martini was thrust into my hand, and I found myself once again on a dance floor, swaying with Jay to Billie Holliday's sultry voice: *Livin' for you, I'm living for you.* Then suddenly, as though a switch had been flipped, the party was over. Everyone had gone. Jay and I were alone. Where was Pat? This was her home, her husband. Why was I still here? I needed to escape, now. But suddenly Jay and I were together, just the two of us, on the massive bed—his wife's bed. I shouldn't be here, I couldn't be here, I must not be here. Jay was married. It was over.

As we made love on top of the down comforter I wondered, where was that lightning bolt that's supposed to strike if you did "it" with a married man? Then came the epiphany: that had never actually been a law, but merely a rule. And rules were made to be broken. Weren't they?

After The Storm

Now that the lightning bolt had failed to materialize, I felt like an egg whose shell had been barely cracked. Might as well open it all the way and let everything pour out. I continued my visits to St. Louis where, if my behavior was designed to rekindle my romance with Jay, it was failing miserably. His marriage to Pat seemed on an even keel and when he noticed me at all, it was to delight in my continued circling of his orbit. My relationship with the Landesmans gave me cachet that I had never before experienced and I seemed to attract men like moths to the proverbial flame. Before long I began an affair with a strung-out, super-talented Beat Poet, one of Jay's close friends.

The poet and I managed a quick trip by coach train to New York, where we stayed with friends of his on the lower east side in a railroad flat. This arrangement was new to this Chicagoan. A series of rooms is laid end to end with no hallway or means of getting from one to the next other than walking through each one. We were given a mattress on the floor of the very first room so that anyone entering by the only door was privy to our arrangement. From there it was a walk through a bathroom, a studio, a storage closet, until at last was reached the coveted rear room with its privacy and its airy windows. In that room resided our hosts— a young newly married artist couple, much in love, secure in the knowledge that their snug nest would not be disturbed. During the two sleepless nights I spent on the floor with the poet I was consumed with jealousy, able to think of little other than the idyllic arrangement and the good fortune of the lovers just three rooms away. How much longer, I wondered, would I be the one in the room that anyone was permitted to enter? That anyone could walk right over?

New York The Hard Way

It's a bright sunny day in Madison and I'm in a booth in the Chocolate Shoppe, still in my cap and gown. Across the table, wearing a dour expression inappropriate to a joyous occasion, sit my mother and father. I'm perspiring, but I don't want to take off the heavy graduation gear. Wearing it keeps me grounded in my identity as a student. Removing it will jolt me into the reality of moving back to the apartment in South Shore Chicago. My eyes dart quickly around the little campus hangout, seeking out familiar faces that could possibly qualify as friends. I have chosen this setting with great care. Although I'm far more comfortable in the Bratskeller, where wine and beer are served, the Chocolate Shoppe captures the essence of all that is wholesome and upbeat and pure about my State University. I wave much too enthusiastically to a pair of old housemates from my dorm days. "Hi, Judy! Hi, Sarah! Come and meet my parents!" Uh, oh. Big mistake. Judy is flashing a large diamond on third finger, left hand.

"Dottie, did you hear the news? Brad is coming home on leave, and we're going to have a wedding before he goes overseas. I'm so excited!"

Mazel-tov, painfully escapes my mother's lips. And our famous hot fudge sundaes arrive.

I gush, "aren't they great? See how they serve the fudge in those little individual pitchers!"

"They do that at Walgreen's too. And their prices are a lot cheaper. And I think their fudge is better. Don't you, Dave?"

"Now, Mom." My father the peacemaker. "She just wanted to show us her favorite place. I think it's terrific the way they've decorated it to look just like a gay nineties saloon."

Actually, the architecture is pure Mission style, but what's a few decades between friends? I let it pass.

I've spilled some gooey second-rate syrup from my pitcher all over the table. It begins to drip dangerously close to my rented robe. As I attempt to swab it with as many paper napkins as I can pry out of the gay nineties napkin holder, the Teaching Assistant from my Restoration Comedy class graces us with a quick stopover, sandwiching us into his table-hoping rounds. In the brief time he's there, my mother manages to give him a quick once-over before launching into her restaurant review. This time my father concurs. It's Walgreens, the winner by a nose. Nerdy though this guy is, I want to die.

Time for us to relinquish our coveted booth, but not before I take the uneaten cherry from my sundae. "Here, Mom. I know you love 'em, even though they probably can't compare to Walgreens."

Even my mother catches my sarcasm. She flashes me a dirty look as we depart in a mood that assures me my calculated choice of location has backfired. Reluctantly I pull off the rented cap and gown, which must be returned by 5 p.m. to qualify for the full refund. The grey

Plymouth is already stuffed with the flotsam and jetsam accumulated during four years of living on my own. Rather than being shipped to a house with a picket fence, it's all going to my parents' neat and orderly two-bedroom apartment. Sure, it's not the scenario they would have preferred, but, Hey Folks, you can't have it both ways. Either you get the college graduate you always said you wanted, or a young knocked-up bride living on an army base. I hand my father the rolled up piece of parchment which he stows carefully in the glove compartment where it will remain until he can get it to a fellow shopkeeper to be Perma-plaqued.

I toss my suitcase onto my old bed where I catch sight of faithful Raggedy Ann, her embroidered smile intact. From there my eye travels to a small pile of mail strewn across my maple desk. On top is an envelope with the unmistaken postmark: Woodstock, New York. Before I can rip it open I confront my mother and give her a piece of my mind: "Mom! Why didn't you tell me I had a letter from Stan? How come you didn't bring this with you to campus?"

"I forgot. So sue me."

I can't rip it open fast enough. It s from Stan Moldawsky, my boyfriend all during my freshman year. Naturally, my parents held no great love for him, having feared that he and I might elope before my finishing my cherished education. The romance had already cooled when Stan was accepted into an Officers Training program and shipped out. We remained close friends, tracking each other often during the following three years. He was as supportive of my plans to go on the stage as was I of his desire for a career in jazz piano. I already knew that Stan was spending his leave at his parents' summer home in the beautiful woods of Woodstock.

*Dear Dottie. Congratulations on graduation. Here is some great news: I've been working with the Woodstock Players and there's a very talented new director here. He's from Panama, — his name is Jose Quintero — a heckuva nice guy. Anyway, his next production is **The House of Bernarda Alba**. It's an all girl cast. I've already told him about you and he says if you come here, there's definitely a role for you. Rehearsals start on the twelfth. How soon can you be here? Let me know right away. Love, Stan.*

My heart was racing, but my head had it beat. I had never heard of this Quintero guy, but I had visited Stan's family at their place in Woodstock, and I knew it was only a couple of hours to Manhattan and Greenwich Village. This was where I belonged! Somehow I had to make it work. My parents leave no room for negotiation: "Oh, no, Young Lady. Don't get any smart ideas in your head. We let you go away those two summers to study with that Erwin Piscator and that was plenty expensive. You're not running off to New York again. You're going to stay right here where you belong."

Here where I belong? I don't think so. Where I belong is in that Number One city with shows and subways and sizzlin' steaks. Where I belong is drinking coffee with actors in the Astor Hotel before making the rounds of casting agents around Times Square. Where I belong is Greenwich Village with artists and poets. Where I belong is window shopping on Madison Avenue, alongside of Greta Garbo, or sitting in the San Remo Cafe sipping wine all night, where I might spot Alan Ginsberg or Delmore Schwartz. Where I belong is where I can be free, free to be me.

I tell myself to calm down, I take a deep breath, and re-read Stan's letter: *rehearsals start on the twelfth.* How could I possibly make it?

Another fly in the ointment. My parents were now in preparation for a cross-country trip to visit their son Alvin, who recently had settled in Los Angeles to work as an accountant. This was a great opportunity for my older brother, whose chronic illness had kept him living at home all during his tenure at the University of Chicago. Everyone had hopes that Alvin would spread his wings on the West Coast, but now there were clues that he was homesick, and my parents worried. They would be gone two weeks. Suddenly the thought of leaving their unpredictable daughter alone in their apartment was anathema. They insisted that I accompany them on their road trip, the last thing I wanted. "You can look for a job when we get back. You're coming with us, and that's final!" My objections fell on deaf ears.

Three overnight stays at Howard Johnson Motels and four National Monuments later we pull up to a converted mansion in the neighborhood just west of downtown L.A. An impressive old three-story Craftsman is now a rooming house for young men on the rise, one of who is my big brother, older by a full three years. My brother and I were barely acquainted. Since grammar school our paths had rarely crossed. Were it not for a physical resemblance, I had often entertained the notion that one of us had accidentally been switched in the nursery. Now he was proudly showing off the room that he shared with a cute young guy from San Diego by the name of Jerry. Hardly my type, Jerry was nevertheless lively and witty and I had no objection when my father invited him to join us that evening for dinner at the Ambassador Hotel. At the end of the evening he took me aside and asked me out for the following night. I readily accepted, the thought of asking permission never crossing my mind. My parents were fine with the idea of their Old Maid daughter having a date, but the following morning when Alvin met us at our hotel, he had cast himself in a new role— Protector of his Baby Sister. Alvin to the rescue! His fury was already unleashed.

"Do, I won't let you be alone with him. You don't know anything about him, but I do. He has no respect for women. I know some of the things he's done with girls. She is NOT going out with that guy."

Who IS this person? I wondered. Could he really be related to me? Just what was it this Jerry kid from San Diego could do to me that hadn't already been done? My parents were caught in the middle, but they chose to side with my brother. I decided to choose my battles. One evening on the town with someone I'd never see again held little or no appeal. For once, I'd play the martyr. "O.K., Al, I don t want to make you unhappy. Please apologize to him for me." I sulked, sure, careful not to overdo it. The calendar was fast accelerating towards to the twelfth of the month; in my busy little brain a plan was hatching. After a day or two as Los Angeles tourists, it was obvious that nobody was having a very good time. As we faced the long return trip to Chicago, I came up with a seemingly spontaneous idea. "Hey, you know what? I really don't feel like being cooped up in the car again. Why don't I just take the train and meet you back in Chicago? That way you can take your time visiting the Steins in Phoenix and I'll be able to hunt for a job before you get back." Nate Stein had been my father's favorite gin rummy partner. Now the gleam in Daddy's eye told me he was badly in need of a gin-fix.

Convincing them was shamefully easy. As they waved good-bye to me at Los Angeles' Union Station I felt like a bird who has been let out of a cage. I settled into a window seat and wrote Stan a letter: *Guess what? I'll be there on the twelfth. Try to meet me at the Greyhound terminal.*

The double lock to my parents' apartment opened easily. Stealthily I made my way to my bedroom, an intruder just passing through. My timing had to be perfectly choreographed. Too soon and they would worry because I didn't answer the phone. Too late, and my window of opportunity would close. Best not to tell anyone, not even Aunt Flo. Though I trusted her implicitly, I knew she would take it on herself to try to talk me out of it. I calculated when Mom and Dad would be crossing Iowa and knew it was now or never. I rewrote the note three times, realizing that it might be my very last communication with my family. I opted for short and sweet. Then I propped it up against their dresser mirror, where they would be certain to see it at once:

Dear Folks: I'm O.K. Don t worry about me. This is something I just have to do. I've gone to New York. Love, Do."

PICTURES

Florence Cohen (Aunt Flo) at 21

Dorothy with her Dad behind their new Plymouth
Chicago 1934

David Saper, New York, NY 1936
The author's father at Rockefeller Center en route
to Boarding *The Normandie* for Europe

Dottie with Stan Moldawsky
Langdon St., Madison, Wisconsin 1943

Rosetta Goldman (Tashka)
Madison, Wisconsin 1945

Dee with Jay Landesman
St. Louis, MO 1947

The author with Cynthia Green Navaretta
Woodstock, NY 1949

Paul and Fred Landesman, London 1961

Dee with Paula Landesman, Paris 1966

Aunt Flo, Uncle Eddie, and Cousin Janet Hoffman
At Farmer's Market, Los Angeles, 1953

PART THREE:
New York, NY

Wrong Turn At Woodstock

In Pennsylvania the bus veered north heading straight for the Hudson Valley, missing New York City completely. Leaving my note, heading downtown and catching a bus, that had all been the easy part. That part was filled with action, with excitement, scary though it was. I had cut the family cord, setting myself free for better or worse. But when the lights were turned off in the Greyhound and the snoring around me became audible, the shock of what I had done hit hard. Would I never see my father or mother again? And was that a good thing? Why was I trembling? Maybe it was just the high air conditioning. I was finally beginning to doze, much the way I did as a little girl in the back seat of our Plymouth during those Sunday drives to visit my cousins in Joliet. Maybe it wasn't as bad as I first thought. My parents would read the note and go crazy at first, but once they saw the reviews of the play, they would understand why I had done what I had done. I could picture it now: *As Adela, the tragic heroine, Dorothy Saper rips at your heartstrings.* The play would be moved to Broadway and one night at curtain call I would spot my mom and dad and brother in the third row, clapping their hands off. Aunt Flo and Uncle Eddie would be beside them, beaming. I would introduce them to the cast, and we would all celebrate afterwards at Sardis before returning to my cozy apartment overlooking the East River. When I jerked awake, my mouth was dry and stale, my clothes rumpled. I dozed again. Now I was in Hollywood, clutching a gold Oscar making my acceptance speech: "…and, of course, to my parents, who never understood me, never encouraged me, who stood in my way as much and as often as possible. See folks, I did it on my own!" Something wasn't quite right. I bolted up, hitting the skinny woman next to me in the arm. As I ran a brush through my frizzy hair I was hit with the realization that it was the thirteenth of the month, which meant that I had missed auditions for *Bernada Alba* by just one day. Hopefully, this new director would be lenient and forgiving. As promised, my former boyfriend Stan met me at the bus terminal and took me directly to the Playhouse, where he introduced me to José Quintero. "Ah, Dottie," said the charming Panamanian, "Stanley has told me so much about you! So you have played Adela in college. Wonderful! Perhaps here you would like to be understudy for such part?" Understudy? What did he mean? I had come clear across the country, I had run away from home to be an understudy? "Well, I was hoping to actually be an actress *in* the play." "But of course! There are many neighbor women. There are several women in mourning. I am sure you will be fine." He handed me a script asking me to read. Humiliated, I repeated the same lines that had been thrown (as a bone to a stray dog) to an entering freshman in our University of Wisconsin production. Glaring at Stan I read: *The sun comes down like lead. I haven't known such heat in years.*

"Excellent, Dottie. Excellent. So I shall expect you here at rehearsal at 8 a.m. tomorrow." And with that he turned away to continue coaching a scene between Bernarda and Poncia. It did little good to reprimand Stan. His leave was at an end; he was shipping out the following day.

Obviously there were more important things on his mind than whether or not his promise of a role in a play had been overblown.

Everyone in this all female cast had already bonded; everyone was familiar with the play. Just like my first day of kindergarten when, starting two weeks late, everyone else already knew the Pledge of Allegiance.

The House of Bernarda Alba opened to big crowds and rave local reviews. As one of the many mourners, needless to say, I was not considered so much as an also-ran, unworthy of even a mention. Nevertheless, Tashka, my friend from school, thrilled that I had finally made it this close to Manhattan, came to have dinner and see the production. I had met her at the end of my junior year at a rally on the steps of the State Capital in Madison. We had taken an instant liking to one another. Tashka had moved to New York almost two years before and had already opened her own bookstore in the heart of Greenwich Village. More than the promise of a Broadway career, she was the strongest reason behind my longing to make it in the Big Apple. Even before my graduation she had been attempting to lure me to the Village and become her business partner. Orphaned at an early age, Tashka had gone through school on scholarships always living on the edge of poverty. Knowing that my father was a successful businessman, she never gave up the hope that perhaps he would become an investor in her shop. The theatre was not really her thing. Now she dismissed the Garcia Lorca play with a wave of her pudgy hand: "Very nice, Do, but what are you wasting your time up here for? You can t really be thinking of spending the whole summer up here! What for? What are you getting out of it? Come to New York, where the real action is. Come now. I need your help in the shop."

She launched into a list of her current lovers and cronies: poets and writers who hung around the store in hopes that their works would be featured in her little window facing Greenwich Avenue, or perhaps that simply by osmosis their writing careers would take off. Or (as I was later to discover) that after closing time Tashka could be persuaded to invite them to spend the night with her on her madras-covered cot in the rear of the shop. Some names I recognized, others I didn't, but they all had a tantalizing familiar ring: Isaac Rosenfeld, Wallace Markfield, Delmore Schwartz, even Anais Nin! "Come now, Do, and you'll meet Anais!" When I momentarily resisted this peer pressure, Tashka played her trump card. She had recently become a devotee of Wilhelm Reich, and was now the proud owner of her very own orgone box. "Don't waste any more time. Pack your bags, and come now!" Surely one of the other mourners could take my lines. They'll never even miss me, I convinced myself. Woodstock had been but a detour. It was time to get down to real life — to making the rounds of Broadway casting directors and drinking the night away with poets and artists in the San Remo Cafe.

I left Jose Quintero's show midway through the run, thus burning one of the most important bridges I might have crossed on my journey to a life in the theatre.

𝒩EW 𝒴ORK, 𝒾'M ℋERE!

So I've arrived. Here I am, living in Greenwich Village, sharing the back room of Tashka's *Four Seasons Bookshop* with a cot, a tiny painted-black bathroom, a hot plate, and her recently acquired orgone box. Occasionally a poet or an artist or a mere acquaintance drops in to sit inside the box. Tashka and I had been friends since my junior year at Wisconsin, and she has finally lost the ability to surprise me. Upon her discovery of Karl Marx, she had traded in her given name, Rosetta, for the more exotic and Russian one she felt better suited her. Orphaned at an early age, she had been allowed to live off campus and thus to have her own kitchen and prepare her own meals. As a Senior, I was now allowed to dine with her. We kicked in $5.00 apiece every week and managed on that to market and cook, alternating duties each week. Needless to say, her meals were far more imaginative, ethnic, and creative than mine. Now after less than a year in business in Greenwich Village, Tash has already begun to cultivate her reputation as Earth Mother. Just like her to have her very own orgone box! Easily impressed by fads and cults, she had already traded in our devotion to Sigmund Freud for the more trendy teachings of Wilhelm Reich, who believed all problems were tied up in the body as well as the mind. The box was specially constructed to build up sexual energy and overcome neurosis. Tashka already credited it with the mild success she was having with boyfriends and business. To me it looked merely like a telephone booth, but who was I to argue with the likes of the writers Isaac Rosenfeld and Saul Bellow, who had came in to try out the box for themselves. As I tossed and turned late one night with my usual insomnia, I could resist temptation no longer. Tiptoeing barefoot on the cold slab floor, I unlatched the door to the mysterious box and willed myself to enter. Once inside I made out a series of baffling levers and wires. I dared not touch or move anything for fear of somehow damaging the precious machine, but I did manage to perch on the little seat inside and inhale deeply. I felt nothing. Nothing. Was I the only person in the Village who had yet to unlock the secrets of its sexual energy, or to experience the big-bang orgasm? I stole back to my little cot, satisfied that I at least had bravely given it a try.

The bookstore comes alive after 5 p.m., when the work force wends its way home or tourists stroll the streets of the Village. I am there punctually to help Tash with the customers and ostensibly to learn the book business which she has accomplished the year before with a stint at the famed *Gotham Book Store*. Working under the tutelage of the foremost barracuda of the retail book trade, Francis Steloff, she has already mastered the art of buying low and selling high by purchasing remainders and used books that can then be marked up to show a profit.

My plan is to spend mornings making the rounds of casting directors and auditions before returning to the shop. But my days are mostly spent apartment hunting. The cot in the rear of the shop can only be temporary. I must soon find comfortable digs out of which to operate and to establish my identity as actress, bookshop partner, and sought-after young intellectual woman-about-town.

Downing a cup of dreadful hot-plate coffee before the shop has opened, I dutifully make my way to the corner newsstand. Then it is time to board the uptown bus that will take me to Times Square, where I will meet with my peers who are exchanging tips on possible acting work. On the bus I pore over the newspaper listings for apartments to rent, apartments to share, apartments uptown, downtown, in Brooklyn, in Queens, Eastside, Westside. There is precious little to scan, and what there is is far too expensive to consider. Finally, my eyes drift down to "rooms to let" — one less appealing than the other. It is wartime. There is a housing shortage. No new buildings have been erected in or around the city for decades. Even with an unlimited income, prospective tenants are forced to wheel and deal for a place to live. Tashka herself had been able to move out of the tiny back room only because, after many months of searching and making contacts, she had secured a sublet from a writer who had taken a job as Sartre's translator in Paris. I had no such luck. My small bank account was dwindling. Surely I would have to contact my parents soon in hopes of replenishing funds, or come crawling back to Chicago with my tail between my legs.

At the drugstore at the Astor Hotel I permit myself another cup of coffee and a piece of toast before red-penciling promising casting calls. Often I bond with other actors (but only if they are not young character ingénues who feel threatened by competition) as we share information while preparing to do rounds of the nearby directors and producers. Their offices are within a few blocks of one another. If there is a potential job it is posted in the *Casting Call* and we are allowed to drop our photos off in hopes of getting an audition. When agents have spare time, they are open to interviewing us if we merely drop in without an appointment. Occasionally there is a cattle call, which means hours and hours of waiting. By rote, and without enthusiasm, I recite my meager list of credits. But my heart isn't in it. I really don't want to go to Kentucky or Tennessee to play one of Snow White's dwarfs with a traveling Children's Theatre Company. I want to stay in the Big Apple, where I belong. First things first. I must get that place of my own! It will be small, but charming. One of the writers will help me erect bricks and boards, which I will fill with periodicals and poetry books. There will be scripts everywhere, thrown casually across the coffee table and in the well-kept bathroom. There will be fresh flowers and bottles of red wine. But first, I must find it! So the "Apartments to Rent" ads in the *Village Voice* are attacked with a determination I had thought would be reserved only for casting calls.

On a Friday morning, a pleasant looking, nicely dressed man sidles up next to me on a stool at the counter, where it's easy enough to strike up a conversation. He tells me that he has recently turned from acting to the production side of show business. We exchange a bit of biography and a few laughs, in other words, we hit it off. Before long, I find myself speaking freely about the bookstore, my leaving home suddenly, and finally, about my experience with the orgone box. As usual when I am relaxed, I come off as witty and enthusiastic. He appreciates me, he understands, he "gets me." My gut feeling tells me that here is an honest guy, a straight shooter. He is to be involved in a new television series that will soon be in production, and he really does believe there may be a role in it for me. "There's a part of a young girl from the Midwest who's a lot like you. I'd like you to meet the producers. They'll be at a meeting with the casting director this evening and if you meet me there I'll introduce you." My heart skips a beat as I hand him my black and white 8" x 10" glossy and my resume'. "Meet me on the N.W. corner of 56th and Broadway, and we'll go up together. I'll be there exactly at 6 p.m. Wear what you're wearing, Dottie. Of course, I can't promise you anything, but I'm sure they'll like you." He scribbles his name, *Richard Morris,* on the back of a menu from the coffee shop, together with the address and appointed time. And he is off.

I race back to the *Four Seasons* to share my excitement with Tashka. She is already holding a feather duster, which she sweeps over the bookshelves. Before I can get the words out of my mouth, Tash beats me to it: "Do, Do, guess what? I have terrific news. I think I've found a sublet for you. At the party last night I met a fellow who lives in a cold water flat on the East side. One of his neighbors has just moved out and the super is going to rent his apartment! You'll have to hurry to meet with him and come up with fifty bucks but if he likes you, you're in! You're supposed to be there tonight as soon as he's off work. Here's the address, show up exactly at six o'clock."

Six o'clock? Tonight? Oh, no! What to do? I explain the dilemma. "Tashka, can't I call him on the phone and change the time? Can't I see him tomorrow morning?"

"Sorry, Do, not a chance. They're already lined up for this. And I don't even have a phone number for him. All I have is the address and his name— Pete." Tashka can't quite grasp the importance of my missing a chance at an acting gig. After all, it was because of her that I had left the Jose Quintero production in Woodstock in the middle of the run. It was because of her that I found myself living in the back of a shop with a cot and a hotplate. How could a long shot at a television role compare with my finding a place of my own? A long shot is what it is, I realize, but the apartment on the East side sounds real. If I get it, I can hope to free myself up to look for much more acting work, possibly even to enroll in the Neighborhood Playhouse, where I can get experience and make valuable contacts.

What to do? How can I reach Richard? There is no phone number on the scrap of paper he has given me. How can I tell him I can't possibly make our 6 o'clock meeting? Do I dare just not show up? How can I stand him up and leave him waiting on a street corner? All the rules of etiquette caution me against it. I'll never be able to face him again if I should run into him. Dare I blow my chances at real work on television?

I grab the telephone book. Richard Morris. Richard Morris. In Manhattan alone there are three full columns with that name. I have no idea where he lives. Desperately, I dial three or four of the "Richards"— two in the 'fifties, one in the 'eighties. No luck. It's useless. No time. I must opt for the apartment. The job will come later. It's time to get dressed and wend my way to the lower east side to meet with Pete.

I make certain to have my checkbook with me, even though my bank balance is pitifully low. Tashka, of course, has so far been unable to pay me in cash for the training and fun I am receiving by working in her shop. The cross-town bus takes me to the bowels of Manhattan. It's an area with which I have had no experience. I follow the directions and walk three long blocks closer to the East River to the address Tash has given me. It is a dilapidated five-story building, but there's a tree in front. There are bars on the windows of what is obviously a basement apartment. I climb the outside flight of broken stairs and locate Pete's name on the dingy mailbox and ring the bell. After what seems an eternity, a sweaty man with curly black hair appears. "You are Dorothy? You want to see the apartment? Yes? Well, did you bring with you the $2,000?"

Two thousand dollars? It might as well be two million. Pete leers at me and invites me to join him in his apartment first. "We might be able to lower the price a little," he says, with a wink of his dark brown eye. I glance at my watch. 6:20 p.m. Even if I were lucky enough to find a taxicab, the earliest I could arrive at 56th and Broadway would be 7 o'clock. Would Richard possibly have waited that long? Too late. I've blown it.

I look up at the disgusting, unappealing man in a dirty T- Shirt emblazoned with a Yankee emblem across the front. Go to his apartment? Perhaps for two rooms with a view in the 'fifties, but a fifth floor walkup with no hot water? No way. "No, thanks, Pete. I don't think I'll be looking at the apartment after all"

Back to Greenwich Ave., where the bookstore is hosting a wine and cheese gathering for a new young writer whose book has just been published. I'm missing out on the audition, sure, but I might still be able to help Tashka pass crackers and meet someone who knows someone who knows someone who has a sublet.

But the cocktail party is sparsely attended, in fact it's about over by the time I return. No likely looking landlords in sight. I see Tashka at the wine bar flirting outrageously with a tall, sandy-haired guy I don t recall meeting before. She rushes over the second she spots me, breathless: "How'd it go, Do?" Not waiting for an answer, she gushes, "I'm glad you're back. Take over and lock up, will you? I'm leaving with Bob— that good-looking guy over there. See you tomorrow." And she's off.

When the last customer has left, I dutifully lock the front door and return to my solitary confinement in the rear, nibbling on leftover cheese as I cross to my little cot. It is late; I am tired and depressed. I open a book of poems written by one of our customers. I squint to read it by the inadequate light that Tash has left behind from the days when she called this her home.

REAL NEW YORKER AT LAST

"NO MEN IN THE room after 11 p.m. and always with the door open." The landlady, print kimono, rollers in hair, might have stepped right out of Central Casting. Her apartment is just inside the outer door near the staircase leading up to my second floor room. She must have had the hearing of a twelve year old, for it was impossible to get through the tiny vestibule without her head poking out. "Yes, of course" I answer. But secretly I can't wait to smuggle a boyfriend upstairs and onto the big iron bed.

O.K., I've finally moved out of my cubby-hole at the rear of the *Four Seasons Book Shop*. I've traded the cot and the hot plate and the orgone box for a shabby front room on the third floor of a converted brownstone on West 73rd Street. It's a long way from the apartment with river view that I had fantasized, but it's wartime, and even for this I had to have a connection. I can't say I'm exactly happy, but I do feel like a real New Yorker at last. Tashka was insistent that I vacate the storeroom in back of the shop and find my own place and this is the best I can do on my limited funds. My room faces the front of the building, which is about the best thing that can be said for it. The iron bed, the mahogany dresser and rickety rocking chair are depressing, but worst of all, the bathroom at the end of the hall must be shared with another tenant— an elderly man with a scruffy grey beard who shuffles to and fro in a worn plaid bathrobe, carrying his shaving brush and mug. I beat a hasty retreat to my room if I see him coming, but I cannot escape the brown stains he leaves in the bottom of the toilet, nor the putrid smell of tobacco or something worse. The ring around the claw-foot bathtub is so uninviting that I prefer sticking to the privacy of my own room, which boasts a small sink. I soon master the art of the sponge bath. I can just imagine my father saying "For this I stood on Ellis Island, for this I broke my back in a men's shop so I could send you away to college? So this is what you want out of life?" Oh, Daddy, Daddy, don't let your heart be broken. This is temporary. I promise I will make you proud of me.

I banish these thoughts from my head as I walk to work. Yes, *walk*, yes *work!* I have a part-time job on west 49th St., and if I am going to become a real New Yorker, I must start to walk and to economize. Because I am not needed in the bookshop until late in the day I was able to accept this job to help out with my mounting living expenses. My friend Geraldine is working as assistant to a Broadway writer-producer by the name of Dale Wasserman, who is in need of someone to type his scripts. Mr. Wasserman was very friendly at my interview, hiring me on the spot. Good thing my typing skills were honed by the many term papers I turned in on deadline during college. So now, instead of doing rounds with other actors, I find myself in a cubby hole in an upstairs office, copying pages of *The Man of La Mancha* as fast as I can. As I insert the blue carbon paper between pages in the huge IBM Electric I allow myself a daydream: wouldn't it be great if Dale Wasserman remembered me enough to offer me a role in his upcoming Broadway production? Even a walk-on would do. I would go on tour with the show, but before leaving New York, one of the featured actresses would fall sick. Dale Wasserman would remember me and bump me up into her role. It's small, but I would stand out. After a tour of the Eastern states we would finally land in Chicago, where my parents would point to me with pride. All of my mother's *Hadassah* friends would attend the Saturday matinee. My mother would accompany them backstage where I would introduce them to the leading man. Only then would they realize that there are more rewarding things in life than a bridal shower or a newborn grandchild. The carbon rips as I try to stuff it through the roller. I'm falling behind and I'm wasting paper. Better stick to business if I don't want to lose this cushy job.

With my first paycheck, I decide to replenish my wardrobe. After all, I barely packed when I fled Chicago which means most of my clothes still hang in my parents' apartment. Tashka has loaned me a few of her dirndl skirts, but they must be turned over several times at the waist. I deserve a dress in my own size. The season has changed, my life has changed, and it is time to investigate the much-heralded Gimbel's on 33 rd Street. I have time for a quick shopping trip before heading to the Village.

Of all the shops on Herald Square, Gimbel's stands out for its huge stock and its reputation for bargains. There is a fluttering in my stomach as I push open the huge swinging door. Chicago, with its neighborhood women's shops and haughty Marshall Field's was never like this. Nor, for that matter, was Madison, Wisconsin where I had clerked two evenings a week during my senior year at a sedate dress shop where the long-sleeved black frock reigned supreme. On emerging from the swinging door I felt like Alice entering a strange land. Clothes were strewn everywhere— on counters, hanging from bare iron racks. And the noise! Half the female population of Manhattan must have found its way to Gimbel's that afternoon. Fighting my impulse to keep right on swinging and exit the front door, I forged ahead. It did little good to ask for help from the women I approached for directions for they all turned out to be customers themselves. Finally I located the size tens. I was in heaven as I scanned the price tags. This was unbelievable, too good to be true. Everything was half as much as I expected.

The Four Seasons Book Shop's cocktail party, which was to launch Anais Nin's new novel, *Ladders to Fire,* was coming up soon. Tashka was working round the clock to make the event a success and I figured this was a good time to launch her new young assistant as well. I would wear something stunning, something outstanding. Not too outstanding I cautioned myself, or it will look as if you are trying to compete with your boss and the guest of honor. Soon my arms were weighted down with potential winners, and suddenly, there it was! No need to look further. Here was the perfect dress — a paprika-colored crepe (one of my best colors.) The shoulder pads gave it an Ann Sheridan look as did the peplums protruding beneath the waist. Time to head for the dressing room, an even greater shock than the store itself. Before I was permitted to enter, a redhead from Brooklyn stopped me: "How many gahments? Too many. You can only bring it foah. Heah, I'll hold these for you." Dresses in hand, I surveyed the scene. Mirror after mirror after mirror, each one with a women in a bra or slip wiggling into a dress in front of it. At the feet of several of them were one or two sniveling, thumb-sucking little kids. A young girl vacated her place and I rushed to hang my *foah* garments and claim the mirror. My slip was none too fresh, but it didn't seem to matter. Modesty was out the window. I tried the paprika first. It was more fitted than it looked on the hanger and seemed a little tight, but I had recently put on a few pounds that I intended to shed. I could scarcely breathe, but I loved it. Taking a cue from others, I turned to the mousy blonde woman next to me. "What do you think of this?" Before she could answer, a buxom Black lady (at least a size 18) was already exclaiming: "Honey that is YOU!" Her friend had other ideas: "Sister, don't you be tellin' that sweet girl to buy that dress. Girlfriend, you wear that dress around a man, and you is just askin' for trouble!" Trouble. That did it. Trouble was my middle name. Trouble was fun. Trouble was just what I wanted. I pulled on my sweater and headed for the long line waiting at the cash register, thrilled to exit the store with a Gimbel's shopping bag, a real New Yorker at last!

The Book Signing

I was late. Tashka had specifically requested me to get to the shop early today as she was expecting an important visitor. Just my luck that Dale Wasserman had given me an extra ten pages of revision on *Man of La Mancha* as I was preparing to leave. He needed them for rehearsal the next day, so there was no negotiation. Now, as I burst through the door to the shop, I saw Tash seated at her desk, deep in discussion with a lovely older woman. The two were conferring earnestly, quietly, sending a clear signal that warned, "do not interrupt." I began alphabetizing the paperbacks, then waited on a customer who requested a copy of Edmund Wilson's *Memoirs of Hecate County.* I wrapped the coveted, banned novel and walked him to the door. Finally, Tashka stood up and only then did she deign to introduce me. The guest was none other than Anais Nin! Of course, I knew that we were planning a cocktail party for the following week to launch the American publication of Nin's latest novel, but her appearance in the store that day was an unexpected treat. Of all the celebrated writers and artists I had met thus far, Anais was surely the most prestigious. She extended her hand and repeated my name in her lovely French/Cuban accent. From an ugly, two-syllable name, it was transformed into a lovely elongated word: *Dor-oh-thee.* A name that for the very first time I was proud to own. My impulse was to repeat: *Ahn-ah-Ees, Ahn-ah-Ees!* I resisted. Instead I mumbled a forgettable, polite, "Nice to meet you." Tashka waved her good-bye with an assurance: "We'll see you next week, and I'll phone your publisher in the morning." Tashka was clearly excited. "Do, this is the biggest coup we've had yet. Anais is autographing her book and speaking only at the *Four Seasons*! She even turned down Francis at the *Gotham Book Mart.* Remind me to call E.P. Dutton first thing tomorrow to make sure we don't run out. We'd better begin shopping for wine and refreshments and spruce up the shop."

The big event was to take place early in the evening on the following Sunday, leaving us only five days to prepare. Good thing I already knew what I was going to wear. My paprika colored crepe dress from Gimbel's was pressed and ready. The excitement of the next few days reached the fever pitch of a pre-wedding celebration. In the back of my mind I remembered that my high-school classmate, Judy Rosenberg, was to be married that same Sunday. My parents were attending the wedding but long ago I had declined the invitation to be a bridesmaid. Handwritten invitations for our autograph party had been mailed to a few select customers and a stack of flyers was placed on our counters. I volunteered for the job of circulating them to other shopkeepers around the Village. "Yes, that's right, Anais herself in person." Or, "What? Don't tell me! You've never heard of Anais Nin?" One of Tash's artist boyfriends had made a spectacular sign complete with Anais' photo that he placed in our front window beneath several copies of her new novel, *Ladders to Fire.* The display had the desired effect: scarcely anyone passed our store without stopping to gape.

Tashka has decided to splurge. Along with several bottles of red wine stand tiny finger sandwiches that she herself created earlier in the day.

I assure myself that their utter simplicity holds far more allure than the champagne and canapés that are being passed this very moment at Chicago's Shoreham Hotel Ballroom, where Judy's Lieutenant has already broken the wine glass. Our event is scheduled for 7 p.m. but by 5 o'clock there is a palpable air of excitement as a few guests arrive early offering to help, or just to gab. It appears that everyone is eager to get close to Nin, that everyone has in some way been affected by her, whether because of her association with Henry Miller or her reputation as the first woman to write pornography. Amazing that the exotic beauty has agreed to just this one book-signing before returning to Europe. Yes, my friend Tashka has scored a real coup all right!

At 6 p.m., utilizing the skills I have picked up as a waitress in Madison, with a flourish of the corkscrew, I open the first bottle of wine. By 7:00 the pile of sandwiches has dwindled. By 7:15 the crowd is getting restless. Tashka and I begin to worry. The small store is jammed packed, so much so that we wonder what space can be found for the guest of honor. We glance at each other across the crowded room, neither of us wanting to entertain the notion that we might be stood up. Not to worry. At precisely 7:30 a dapper editor from the Dutton Publishing House arrives with the charismatic Anais Nin in tow. She slithers in wearing a floor length but understated light grey chiffon with a matching stole that she drapes gracefully across her shoulders. Moving slowly, she makes her way through the crowds, smiling graciously. Tashka plants a light kiss on her cheeks before leading her to the desk that has been set up with piles of the hardcover book. Quickly a line forms shoving cash at Tashka, who makes change from a little tin box. The party is already a success, judging by the money changing hands and the good spirits, enhanced no doubt by the consumption of red wine and the unusually strong but not unpleasant aroma from the passing of skinny, hand-rolled cigarettes. At last Anais stands and begins to speak in her melodious continental accent. Briefly she addresses her body of work that has led up to this latest novel about love between the sexes. But of course, it is about Henry and June Miller that the crowd wishes her to speak. Although she politely declines, there is a round of applause, and then the formal part of the evening gives way to a party atmosphere. My bartender duties over, I now have leave to circulate. The room is so crowded that I find myself shoved against the bookshelves on the back wall of the shop with scarcely room to breathe.

Among all the attractive men there, only one truly captures my interest. He is Kevin, the older brother of my close friend from college, Cynthia. I have harbored a secret crush on Kevin for years. Of course, I realize he is a homosexual, and he has always adopted the role of mentor, treating me like his baby sister. Kevin knows everything about all the arts, mainly the ballet. In New York he is considered a certified balletomane. Rumor has it that he was briefly married to a young ballerina who died in a plane crash, although I have never been able to confirm this with Cyn. In any case, I find Kevin the most attractive, sexy, witty, intriguing man I know. Short in stature, dark wavy hair, always dressed impeccably, he has the look I love. His delightful, wicked sense of humor is irresistible. Now, across the room, he sends me a mischievous wink. A moment later I find him pressed closely to me against the wall, where we share a laugh, Between the wine, the fumes from the strange cigarettes, the excitement of the moment, I am feeling no pain. Then I realize that Anais is also standing close to me on the other side. I catch a whiff of her exotic French perfume as I try to eavesdrop on her conversation with the man on her right. Now I am aware that Kevin has pressed up tight against me, his pants rubbing the skirt of my Gimbel's dress. What is that hard lump I feel? Can it be possible? Of course it can—why not? Isn't it true that Kevin likes women as well as men, and that the right woman (me) could turn his supposed homosexuality around? Fleeting fantasies of a future with Kevin find their way to my brain as I feel something soft caressing my right shoulder, making its way down my arm. I don't have to turn my head to know that this seductive gesture is coming from none other than Anais Nin. So, everything they say about Henry Miller and June and Anais must be true. Suddenly my possibilities seem limitless. What happens now? Is the next move up to me? The decision is taken out of my hands as Kevin turns to embrace an old friend and Anais moves quickly away to greet her translator.

The party winds down as the literati move to the door clutching their autographed first editions. I am so tired I decide to spend the night on my old cot in the back of the shop, but I discover I am too late. Two young women are casually draped over a young bearded man, all three sound asleep. I have no choice but to catch the subway uptown to 72nd. Street to my dingy rooming house.

I am completely sober by the time my head hits the pillow. My old pal, insomnia, returns, only tonight it is worse than ever. A sour taste rises up in my throat as I picture my parents enviously watching Judy Rosenberg being tossed into the air on the wooden chair reserved for Jewish brides. Despite myself, I must have dozed off for a moment, for I could swear I hear Aunt Flo s voice: "What are you doing there, Kiddo? You know you don't want Kevin and for sure you don't want Anais. Tashka will never make you a partner in the Book Shop—you're skinnier and prettier and she knows it. She made promises that she isn't going to keep and she made you blow any chance you might have to get cast by Jose Quintero. You don't belong in New York! It s time to come home to your nice clean bed." Was this why I tossed and turned all night? Or was it all that wine and pot? Or could it be because my period was three weeks late?

BIG FIX IN BROOKLYN

OF COURSE THERE WAS no way of knowing for certain, but all the signs pointed in one direction. I had never been this late before. Long hot soaks in the dreaded bathtub of my rooming house failed to trigger my period. It took only a few seconds upon awakening each morning for the chilling reality to sink in: I was pregnant. Where could I turn? My friend Geraldine, a playwright, was immersed in the off-Broadway theatrical scene and knew everything about everything. It was she who had arranged for my job transcribing for Dale Wasserman. Three years my senior, she immediately set about taking me in hand. "Don't worry, Do. Sure, it's illegal but there's a guy I heard about over in Brooklyn who asks no questions and doesn't charge too much. I'll take you there myself."

Bless Geraldine. I had never felt so alone. No need to discuss this with any of the guys I had known. They would insist it was my responsibility, which, indeed, it was. Why had I drunk so much wine on so many nights, and how could I have been so careless? I had no one to blame but myself. With Geraldine making all the "arrangements" I put myself in her hands.

On the appointed day Gerry met me at the 72nd St. Subway station where we descended the long staircase as she guided me to the train that would take us to Brooklyn. We switched trains on 42nd St., shuttling across tracks to catch the Express. Brooklyn. A foreign land. My sojourn in New York had only once before taken me across the Bridge when I had attended a concert at the Brooklyn Museum. Now the IRT Express sped past unfamiliar signs leading deeper and deeper into the heart of that borough. Eastern Parkway. Prospect Park, Church Avenue. I imagined thugs on every corner brandishing switchblades as they made snide remarks. "Hey, goily, wheah ya goin', huh?" When we at last would reach our destination it would no doubt be a run-down tenement much like the one where I had encountered Pete, the super with an apartment to let.

Still trembling, I perked up at the sight of a familiar name: *Brighton Beach*. Next stop was *Ocean Parkway* and it was here that Geraldine stood up. "O.K., Do. This is it. Hang on to your purse."

Up a steep flight of stairs, through a turnstile, and out to whatever fate held in store. I blinked. Surprisingly, the sun was shining brightly. It was still early morning. The street was wide and clean, a leafy parkway running down its center. "Ocean Park Blvd." On one side sat a row of well-kept shops. "Appetizing" said the first. What was sold in there? I assumed the owner had meant it to read "Appetizers" but had somehow misspelled the word. Next to it a shopkeeper was setting out row upon row of brightly colored fresh fruits and vegetables. In a bakery window sat an array of fresh rolls and an assortment of Danish pastries. Smiling matrons pushing large blue baby carriages, were beginning to shop. Everyone seemed to be going about their business as though this was just an ordinary day.

It was only one block before Geraldine held up a slip of paper with the address. "O.K. here we are." Geraldine must be mistaken, for this was a pleasant large, well-kept brick apartment building with a wide driveway encircling a courtyard. A double door opened into a tiled lobby with a bank of three elevators at its rear. Next to the elevators appeared tasteful silver plaques with names engraved in block letters: Paul Strassberg, DDS, Eric Horowitz, Pediatrics. And underneath, the name we were seeking: J.R. Liebman, M.D. Suite. 212. Still holding my hand and oozing confidence, Geraldine pushed the button in the elevator to the second floor. There was no turning back.

A crisply-uniformed nurse behind the desk smiled slightly as she asked my name. Quickly the well-rehearsed pseudonym sprang to my lips: "Doris Sappington." Then, far too casually, she inquired as to whether I had brought the envelope. Satisfied that it contained the correct amount of cash, she led me through a door, presented me with a gown and slippers, introducing me finally to the elderly, gravel-voiced Dr. Liebman.

After being allowed to rest on a clean white cot for a while, the nurse assured Geraldine that it was O.K. for us to wend our way home. With Gerry taking my arm, we slowly walked the block to the subway station that would deposit me on 72nd Street. Back in my own neighborhood, with a huge weight off my shoulders, I felt positively euphoric. Before returning to my rooming house I insisted that Gerry allow me a brief stop to treat her to a cup of coffee After tucking me into my big iron bed, satisfied that I was all right, my dear girlfriend tiptoed out, leaving me to fall into the most peaceful sleep I had known in weeks.

PART FOUR:
...And Beyond

THE FAMOUS VIOLINIST

FAILING TO LAUNCH A career or a bright future in New York City my only option was to return to my parents' apartment in South Shore. After knowing several years of freedom, the constraints were suffocating. My trips to St. Louis continued. Paula had been correct: Jay's marriage did not mark the end of the world, merely of an era. Weekends in St. Louis provided the escape I needed.

Each visit was like the breaking open of a piñata, with brightly colored surprises spilling out. Saturday nights were unpredictable and always exciting, but nothing could surpass the Landesman annual New Year's Eve party, which had already become a tradition. The party began with a scavenger hunt—a scavenger hunt like no other. Two teams were selected and given a list which included esoteric clues leading to seemingly unattainable treasures. Being on the same team with Jay permitted me close proximity for the entire night. (Be still, my heart!) We fanned out across the unfamiliar old city early in the evening, reassembling at dawn, where prizes were awarded and the New Year was ushered in with Bloody Mary's and champagne.

My birthday falls just three days after New Years, and the year I was to turn twenty-one Paula and Fred insisted I remain with them to celebrate. Among my frequent escorts was a popular columnist for the St. Louis Post Dispatch. That week he was to interview the rising young violinist who was to be soloist with the St. Louis Symphony Orchestra. A child prodigy whose parents had emigrated from Russia, the already-famous violinist was said to be one of the most gifted to ever hold the instrument. We were to attend his concert, joining him for dinner later.

We had third row center seats for the symphony, where the already famed musician (who shall hereafter be referred to simply as F.V.) would wow the audience with his playing of the *Mendelssohn Concerto in B*. The late supper took place in the sumptuous dining room of the Park Plaza Hotel, a far cry from my campus Bratskeller or a Greenwich Village hangout. An audible buzz preceded the F.V. as he made his way to our table. After a triumphant concert, he was exhausted, elated, and definately hungry. The chubby musician could sure pack it away. Between bites he chatted with his reporter buddy until, sated at last, he wiped his sensuous lips on the linen napkin, and turned his full attention to the brunette on his left. On learning it was my Big Birthday, he raised his glass in a toast. "Twenty-one? You're a mere baby." He himself was already twenty-six, almost twenty-seven. Now he seemed enchanted, wanting to know everything about me, including my current address. Never one to embroider a resume', I was up front about my limited knowledge of classical music. That was just fine with him, he promised to teach me everything I needed to know, beginning the following week, when he was to perform with the Chicago Symphony Orchestra. My ticket would be waiting at the box office and a backstage pass would be arranged for after the concert.

The reporter soon faded into the woodwork, excusing himself when F.V. assured him he would see me home.

My heart was thumping as I felt his arm around me during the limousine ride back to Paula and Fred's. Was this actually happening? Could he really be interested in me? When we pulled up at what I thought to be the impressive old mansion on Westminster Place, F.V. not too politely declined my invitation to come in and meet my hosts and see their house. "No thanks, I've seen houses. I'll see you backstage in Chicago on Thursday." The limo sped away. Paula, waiting up like a mother hen, clucked and crowed over my triumph. "You see, Dee, I promised you there was life after Jay!"

My Musical Education

"WHERE ARE YOU GOING all dolled up like that?" My mother demanded to know. How could I tell her the truth: I was headed downtown to Orchestra Hall to attend a concert in which famed violinist Isaac Stern would be soloist with the Chicago Symphony Orchestra. My ticket was waiting to be picked up at the box office. After the concert I was to be admitted backstage, where Isaac would be waiting to take me to supper and (it was understood) back to his hotel room. My parents had only been in Orchestra Hall a few times in their lives, and certainly never backstage. The idea was beyond their comprehension. How could I let them know? How could I expect them to share in my enthusiasm? Even if I did, there was a nagging feeling of unreality about the evening. Sure, Isaac had telephoned me that afternoon to confirm plans, yet inside of me hung the suspicion that the whole thing had been a colossal sham, a huge mistake, a cruel joke. There would be no ticket waiting for me, I would slink back home by myself. So I chose the easy way out: I lied.

114

"I'm meeting Bunny and we re going to the concert together. If it s too late to come home, I'll just stay downtown in her apartment at the Stage Club. Don't wait up for me—see you tomorrow!"

Well, it was only half a lie. My friend Bunny had been admitted to the residential hall for actresses on the Near North Side. She had, indeed, given me an open invitation to spend the night there and once or twice I had already taken her up on it. But I would not be there tonight. What if my parents called to check up on me? I found a pay phone before boarding the I.C. train for The Loop and reached Bunny to warn her to cover for me. Although I was ushered to a fifth row center seat, I found it hard to relax and lose myself in the music for fear of being caught. That is, until Isaac Stern made his appearance as soloist. Again, as in St. Louis, he was to play the Mendelssohn Concerto, only this time I was truly overwhelmed. How could these magnificent sounds be emanating from this short pudgy little man — a man who had taken a personal liking to me?

An usher helped me find the stage door where I was immediately admitted. There stood Isaac amidst a throng of admirers. His quick glance warned me not to interrupt. I stood helplessly by, shuffling from foot to foot. As I was contemplating a hasty retreat, I was stopped by a charming silver-haired pixie of a man. "Aha! You must be Dee, about whom I have heard so very much." I failed to recognize Stern's longtime accompanist, Alexander Zakin, who ordered me at once to address him by his Russian name, *Shura*. He ushered me into the privacy of Isaac's dressing room, where we waited for His Lordship's fans to leave. In those few moments, he forever endeared himself to me. In his warm, open manner, *Shura* described his relationship with the prodigy. More than simply an accompanist, he played the role of a loving surrogate father. When at last I left the theatre on Isaac's arm, he called after him, "Ah, Itzak, this one you must not let get away!"

My parents need not have worried. I did indeed go to Isaac's hotel room, but it was not precisely for the reason they might have feared. In spite of a long day and evening, the virtuoso was not ready for bed. Instead, he was anxious to show me the precious instrument he had recently acquired. By dubbing the music for a film, he had earned enough money to purchase a rare Guarnarius violin. I had seen the film *Humoresque* because I knew Clifford Odets wrote the screenplay. John Garfield played the lead role of a prizefighter-turned-violinist. Isaac's hands were superimposed on Garfield's and he had coached the actor to appear to be playing. It was the strains of music coming from Stern's violin that helped make the movie a hit. Now at midnight, back in his hotel room, still exhilarated from his performance, he put the Guarnarius under his chin, clasped his hands around its neck, and drew the bow across the strings. His eyes closed as he worked his way lovingly through the entire score of the film. Occasionally he would move gracefully from bedroom to dressing room and back. As one hand ran the bow across the strings, the other held the neck in a loving embrace. Pluck, pluck, pluck, went his stubby fingers. As I listened I longed for those hands and fingers to play my body, as they were the Guarnarius. The music made me want to move—to dance. My body took on a life of its own as I began a series of modern dance movements in time with the strains of *Humoresque*. Gradually I shed my clothes until I was performing completely in the nude. From the corner of my eye, I caught Isaac's approving glance. Surely this would be enough to encourage him to put down the Guarnarius and turn his attention to his own personal instrument. It was not to be—at least not that night. Isaac Stern had exhausted his lovemaking capital. He tenderly replaced the priceless violin in its velvet-lined case, falling on his pillow exhausted, beckoning me at last to join him. But before I could snuggle into the crook of his arm, the Famous Violinist was deep in the arms of Morpheus, snoring the gentle snore that he had so richly earned.

ᎩELLOW ᏚILK ᏢAJAMAS

AFTER THAT FIRST NIGHT with Isaac the relationship took on a life of its own, its pattern governed, of course, by the Celebrity. There was no talk of love or commitment but a warm and relaxed friendship began to grow. A tacit understanding came about that whenever he was playing in or near Chicago, we would be together. The F.V. made no attempt to conceal my identity. On the contrary, I was introduced to everyone in the music world, almost flaunted as a trophy on his arm. What the prodigy lacked in looks he compensated for in charm and personality and brains. He attracted a large circle of admirers because of his warmth, his outspoken liberal political stance, and his depth of knowledge in far ranging areas. Whatever musicians happened to be in town were drawn to him. I was often included. There would be lunches and dinners, but mainly there would be music. At the drop of a hat, Gregor Piatagorsky, premier cellist in the world, would sit down to play a duet. Then there was the piano virtuoso Artur Rubenstein, or the wheelchair-bound gifted violinist Itzak Perelman. Eugene Istomin would often appear, as would Leonard Rose or William Kappel. On one memorable evening we all gathered at a large round table to toast Rubenstein on the birth of his new son, John. Rubenstein was radiant after speaking by phone to his adored wife, Nadia. It had been twenty years since the birth of their last child, making the pianist the butt of much good-natured teasing.

My favorite night by far was the one during which there was excited talk of "Lennie"— for Leonard Bernstein was in town. Before I knew it we had all piled into a taxi and hustled to his suite at the Ambassador East Hotel. Piatagorsky knocked, the door burst open and there, welcoming the heavyweights of the music world, stood the young Adonis himself, garbed in canary yellow silk pajamas. Wavy black hair flowing, his handsome face broke into a wide grin that included even an unknown young girl from South Shore.

"Welcome! Come in, come in, my friends!"

Behind "Lennie" appeared a long, shiny black Steinway piano, the kind ordinarily reserved for the stage of a concert hall. Soon, without too much coaxing, Bernstein sat down at that piano to treat us to his own already familiar rendition of George Gershwin's *Rhapsody in Blue*. Electricity filled the room. When he smiled at me as he reached the end, I absorbed not just the music, nor his mane of hair, but those electric-yellow silk pajamas. Not too much later, I would see him performing this piece on television, or witness him instructing young people in the art of the orchestra, or constantly hear the strains of his masterpiece, *West Side Story*. Whenever possible I watched him conduct a full symphony orchestra wearing black tie and tails. But if he had asked me, my advice would have been for him to perform in nothing other than a pair of canary yellow silk pajamas.

RUNNING AWAY
FROM HOME (AGAIN)

WHILE LOOKING FOR MORE glamorous employment, I had been reduced to giving acting lessons to the neighborhood kids in our family living room. *Merde,* I thought in the middle of the class, Cee-Cee rang the bell early and I never took my diaphragm off the bathroom sink! "Cee-Cee, I'll be right back. Keep practicing your breathing lessons." Racing to the rear of the long apartment, I hope against hope that my mother had not yet returned from shopping, that there is still time! Nope, too late. Mom was just hanging up the kitchen phone, an expression of gloom on her face. "Your father is on his way home, Young Lady. Finish up the lesson and then come right back here."

"Cee-Cee I've got a terrible headache. Afraid we'll have to cut the lesson short today. See you next week, Honey. Be careful crossing the street on your way home."

In my room, I soon realize that my mother has not only seen the incriminating evidence (which I foolishly had left out to dry) but had found time to sneak a glance at a half finished letter to Cynthia, carelessly left open on top of my maple desk. Just like her! I m not surprised. So this was it. The end of life as I had known it. Here I was, a twenty-one year old college graduate, feeling like an alien on a foreign planet. This was 1948. Twenty-one year old girls were not supposed to be single— they were supposed to be married, preferably to a G.I serving overseas, to whom they would write lengthy letters three times a week as they volunteered at the Red Cross, awaiting the birth of their first baby.

There was no way I could face my father. Never. Never again. Quickly, with no hesitation, I tossed a few clothes into a brown paper grocery bag, rifled through my dresser drawer for what little cash was there, slipped on a lightweight black coat and grabbed my purse, careful to check for my driver's license and social security card. Functioning with remarkable calm, not unlike a survivor of a catastrophic disaster, I quietly shut the front door behind me and hurried down the stairs.

The Illinois Central commuter train ran downtown every twelve minutes. If I hurried I could catch the next one, beating Daddy to the house. Best to walk a block out of the way to avoid running into him as he pulled his car into the alley behind our building. In a few moments, I would have left South Shore behind forever. The cashier in the booth shoved my one-way ticket to the Loop into my fingers just as the Express train pulled up. Panting, I took a window seat where I could watch my past life whiz by. *Farewell, South Shore Drive* (sandy beaches, white caps, bike paths). *Goodbye, Morton's Restaurant* (after-prom hamburgers, gin-and-tonics), *So long, Donnelly's Printing Company* (giant, grimy behemoth, birthplace of Chicago's *Yellow Pages*). This would be my final glimpse of these familiar landmarks. Saturday after Saturday, year after year, I had ridden this route for drama lessons on the fourth floor of the Baldwin Piano Building on Van Buren and

Wabash. And for what? To teach six year-olds like Cee Cee to curtsy and enunciate.

Exiting now at the Monroe Street station, some unknown force propels me down the five blocks west to the Greyhound Bus Terminal. How do I even recall where it is? Never before had there been occasion to go inside. The dirt on the white tile floor repels me, as do the ragged men and women, several of whom are sound asleep on the heavy mahogany benches. A bulletin board above the ticket window clicks off arrivals and departures. Just a little over an hour before the next bus to St. Louis. Should I buy my ticket now? Take a breather, wash up first. Should I telephone Paula in St. Louis to let her know I am on my way? Not necessary, really. That would mean changing a bill into silver and eating up a lot of precious cash. There is no doubt that I'll be welcomed at Paula and Fred's. There's plenty of room in their big old Victorian House on Westminister Avenue, and though Baby Rocco has yet to sleep through the night, they'll be delighted as always. It occurs to me that this time might be different, when they realize I'll be staying in St. Louis for good. I'll have to get a job of course, and after that a place of my own. No time for doubts. No choice. I've got to get out of here. This is Chicago, and in the entire city there is no one who speaks my language. Well, that s not entirely true. There is ONE person — Aunt Flo.

Should I even involve Flo? My parents will surely telephone her. They might even call the police! That's the last thing I need. The big round terminal clock shows that it is the middle of the afternoon. Barely an hour had passed since this whole nightmare began. Flo would still be at work at the publishing company on the Near North Side. Luckily the telephone number is in the little black address book tucked into the bottom of my purse. The accordion glass door to the telephone booth slides shut; I dial the number and drop a nickel into the slot. "Hello, Flo? It's me. Have they called you yet? Do you know anything? Good...I just want to tell you that I'm O.K. I'm fine. I'm at the Greyhound station and I'm leaving in a few minutes for St. Louis. Flo, I'm never coming back. I can't. Don't try to talk me out of it. I just didn't want you to worry. When you hear from them tell them I'm safe. I'm all right. That's all I can say now." Flo's voice is steady: "Listen, Kiddo, I'm leaving here right now and I can be there in twenty minutes. Wait for me. Just don't get on that bus. I won't try to talk you out of anything, but just promise me that you'll wait there for me. Promise? Wait!"

"All Aboard for Springfield and St. Louis. All Aboard!" The bus pulls away just as Flo bursts through the double doors. "Let's get out of here. There's a place around the corner for coffee."

Over coffee and a stale Danish, the words come gushing out. It was always easy to tell Flo everything.

"O.K., Kiddo, I understand just how you feel and I don't blame you, but St. Louis isn't going anywhere. It'll still be there tomorrow or the next day. Come home with me tonight. Sleep on it. We won't even try to explain anything to Eddie if you don't want to."

"I can't, Flo. I just can't ever face them again. I've got to get away now. I can't stay in Chicago one more day! You promised you wouldn't try to talk me out of it."

Flo plays her trump card: "Listen to me. I'm going to tell you something now that I never told you before and I was sure I never would. What you don't know is that the day you scattered rose petals at my wedding to Eddie, it wasn't the first wedding I ever had. There was a boy. We were high school sweethearts and we were very much in love. We were in our senior year and we were both seventeen. His parents didn't think I was good enough for him. They decided they would break us up once and for all, so they bought a business out in California and were going to move out there with him when he graduated. We couldn't stand the thought of being separated so we figured the only way we could stay together was to get married. We snuck off to Michigan, where it was legal. We stayed away for two days. You can imagine what happened

122

when we go back! His mother and father locked him in the house. They got a lawyer and had the whole thing annulled. Two weeks later he was on a train for Los Angeles. I've never seen him again. We sneaked in some phone calls and letters and he even sent me a ticket for California, but I never had the nerve to use it. I was so ashamed. And I guess part of me still is. My Pa had his stroke a few weeks later. Your mother'still holds it against me." Flo s voice grew softer.

An annulment? Wasn't that only for Catholics? Does that mean that while Aunt Flo was still in high school she had "done it?"

"Gosh, Flo. I can t believe it! Does Eddie know?"

"I kept it from him for a long time. I knew I couldn't marry him until I came clean. That was one reason we were engaged so long. He's O.K. with it now, but we never mention it. It's still a deep dark secret, but I figured you should know. I'm telling you now so you'll realize that everything changes and calms down if you give it enough time.

I finish my black coffee and allow myself to be led to the "El" that takes us to the West Side. The moment we get in the house, Flo telephones her sister Lily. "She's here. She's safe. She's all right. She doesn't want to talk right now."

I remain in the little apartment on the West Side with my aunt and uncle and little Eugene and Janet a full week. "Take your time," they assure me, "you can stay here as long as you want."

At the end of the week, my father, the well-groomed haberdasher, looking ashen and somewhat older, arrives by appointment for a private meeting, to cut a deal. Flo takes the kids to the park so there will be peace and privacy. The Beau Brummell of South Shore looks seriously at his daughter. This is the deal: if I will agree to move back home and pick up a semblance of a normal life, neither he nor my Mom will ever mention the past or the incident again. In that way, the family reputation will remain clean, his business will not suffer, nor will his standing as President of the Men's Club at his synagogue. There's more: "I'm going to deposit $5,000 into a bank account in your name. You can do whatever you choose with it: you can buy a mink coat or take a trip to Europe, or go to a (he gulps slightly, trying to get his tongue around the unfamiliar word) psychiatrist. As long as you keep it quiet around the neighborhood." The deal is sealed. Flo returns from the park, and everyone agrees it would be best if I return to the South Side the following day.

I telephone my little students to say they can resume their lessons. I know what my next call must be. I lower my voice as I dial the Psychoanalytic Institute.

BRAVE NEW WORLD

SEVERAL MONTHS INTO OUR relationship, Isaac, the Famous Violinist, had surprised me by taking me to a party in the North Shore suburb of Winnetka at the home of his sponsor, Max Adler. I was all too familiar with the name, having spent countless hours in the awesome museum on the lakefront that bore his name. With its amazing exhibits of stars and planets it had always been the favorite of my many Chicago field trips. I was cautioned to be on best behavior, for the Adler family was an important part of his life. The multi-millionaire philanthropist was married to Sophie Rosenwald, heir to the Sears Roebuck fortune and they were partial sponsors of Isaac's meteoric career.

Whenever we were guests at the Adler estate, Isaac was immediately swept away, always the center of attention. Perhaps because I looked nervous and lost, I was soon taken under the wing of the youngest Adler son, John. Johnny Adler was dark and handsome and only a few years younger than I and we seemed to feel a genuine connection. We talked on the phone frequently and several times we met for coffee in the loop after one of Johnny's psychoanalytic sessions. This was 1948. Psychoanalysis was in its infancy. The very word carried with it an exotic, mysterious aura. Johnny was the first person I had personally known who was deep in the throes of a bona fide "analysis." With his unlimited income, of course, he accepted it as something one pursued as a matter of course. He urged me to investigate it as a tool towards a happy life.

Due to Johnny's teachings, I knew that in order to engage a psychotherapist, one needed a referral. This could be obtained only by going through a "Psychoanalytic Institute." Chicago boasted two such Institutes, of opposing schools. The first, the Jungian, named for its famous founder, Carl Jung, carried on his teachings after he had broken ranks with his original mentor, Sigmund Freud. The second was simply called, "The Freudian Institute." I opted for the latter.

Had I been inquiring about the name and address of a bank to rob, the voice at the other end of the phone could not have been more guarded. I was told that because many doctors had not yet returned from active military duty there was a serious shortage of M.D's, particularly Psychiatrists. After an initial intake, I was given, with great reluctance, the names of two possible candidates.

"No, no, no," blurted the first, "I have no time; absolutely no time at all."

My ever-present fear of rejection blossomed in full force. I forced myself to dial the second number.

The voice was warm, friendly, non-threatening. It might have belonged to my Uncle Eddie. Relief washed over me.

"You want to make an appointment? Yes, I think I can see you. Would you like to come in on Monday? Could you make it downtown by 8:00 a.m.?"

I still harbored secret hopes of being on a bus bound for St. Louis. By Monday morning I had thought I would have left Chicago behind forever. Out of the corner of my eye, I could see my Aunt Flo busying herself in the kitchen as I cupped the mouthpiece of the black telephone and in a hushed tone assured him that I would be there. St. Louis could wait!

At precisely 8:00 the following Monday morning I entered a wood paneled waiting room overlooking Lake Michigan. The doctor himself opened the door to his consultation room with a warm, welcoming smile shining beneath his rimless spectacles.

"Come in. Let me hang up your coat. Have a seat over there."

Motioning to the beige sofa he seated himself in what was obviously the Psychoanalyst's sacred chair. This placed us approximately three feet apart. It was still wartime. Real estate was high. Space was at a premium.

Gazing right into my face: "You're very attractive. Why are you here?"

Attractive? Me? With my bushy hair and wide nose? I had rarely been told I was attractive and certainly never felt it. Was this a ploy to build up my self-esteem? Even if true, did that mean I had no need of therapy? Was this an appropriate comment to make to a patient? Would Sigmund Freud approve? Had a boundary already been crossed? Greene was waiting for an answer, and it took no more than a few seconds to blurt out my problems with my parents, and a good chunk of what I viewed as my sordid past.

Satisfied that here was a young woman in need, the doctor agreed to begin my treatment four times a week, Monday through Thursday, at 8 a.m. Thus began my Freudian journey.

ARGYLE SOCKS

AFTER SEVERAL WEEKS OF therapy, I was accustomed to stretching out lengthwise on the beige sofa, my head raised on a small pillow. Dr. Greene's chair was placed behind, just out of my line of vision and thus I was deprived of any change of expression he might subconsciously have shown. Since the office was so tiny, my analyst's crossed feet were but a few inches from my right eye. Absorbed though I may have been in my own thoughts, I was equally aware of Greene's shiny black loafers and the socks rising above them. Day after day, his feet were encased in a pair of colorful, argyle socks. Conservative dresser that he was, the socks seemed his only telltale indulgence. Red/black/grey. Tan/green/brown. Magenta/gold/grey. Big, beautiful diamond shapes of powder blue, navy blue, beige, turquoise, rust, pewter. How many pairs could he possibly own? It was enough to make me lose my train of thought.

My therapy progressed. Adoration for my father was gradually replaced by understanding and empathy for my mother. Since I had always played the role of Daddy s Little Darling, it was only natural for Mom

128

to feel excluded, hurt, and resentful. Added to that was my intense friendship with her youngest sister Florence—my Aunt Flo. The day of this epiphany, the socks were a startling electric blue and yellow, bright as a flashing neon sign. Next came the sorting out of explanations for my promiscuity, for the sabotaging of my career, the confusion over Jay and St. Louis, and finally, my ill-fated affair with Isaac Stern (aka, Famous Violinist). Since Greene himself played the violin, this relationship, the one that had directly triggered my entering analysis, was accorded time and-a-half. Was it my imagination, or were the socks always brown on the days devoted to the F.V.? A magical force seemed to propel the analyst into wearing the color that best suited the mood of my kick-start dream. Some mornings, riding the Illinois Central train to his office, I would play a guessing game as to the color of Greene's socks, often betting against myself. My high batting average amazed me!

As Christmas approached, even I could tell that I was moving forward. I had a real job teaching creative dramatics in a prestigious pre-school, I was acting with a professional theatre troupe, and my mother and I were even taking occasional shopping trips together! True, Dr. Greene was being paid, but there must be some other way to express my gratitude. A gift was in order, no doubt about it. It required little thought to come up with the perfect idea: a pair of stunning argyle socks. They must be very classy, as befits a Freudian Analyst, while at the same time they should express the spirit of the season. Nothing would do but a distinctive argyle pattern in the Christmas colors of red and green.

My father had sold socks in his men's shop for over twenty years. His merchandise was well priced and attractive but often boring, the sock case revealing neat rows of black or navy blue lyle. Not a pair of argyles among them, but even if there had been, this was to be a very special, private gift purchased with my own money. Although it was an unwritten law in my house that we were never to enter the men's department of Marshall Field and Co., the week before

Christmas found me strolling those aisles. I knew I should be helping my mother as cashier in our own store, but pursuing my mission was more important.

"May I help you?" Came the question from a voice tinged with a steely British accent. My request for a pair of argyle socks in Christmas colors was met with a thinly disguised sneer.

Out came a garish pair suggesting Halloween rather than Christmas. The red was nearly a bright orange, and the opposing kelly green would work for St. Patrick's Day.

"No, no. Isn't there something more subtle than these?"

"Yes, we do have one pair you might like, but of course they are made of pure cashmere, and I m afraid they are rather costly."

"That's all right. Please let me see them."

The Sneer bent down, slowly sliding open a drawer that might have contained rubies and emeralds. Inside lay several pairs of cashmere socks, one more beautiful than the other. Only then did I understand why my eyes had fastened day after day on Dr. Greene s socks. Of course! They were all pure cashmere!

I fingered through a small pile before spotting the perfect gift! My fingers ran over the sumptuous fabric woven in Santa's favorite colors— a luscious shade of deep red contrasted with a rich green diamond, held together with a crisscross line of black. How proud Dr. Greene would be to show them off on Christmas day! "From a young patient," he would admit, "a very special patient." Here was a gift that said, "Thank You," and beyond that, perhaps even, "I Love You," for after all, my transference had begun.

Using my recently acquired Marshall Field charge card, I completed the transaction. There remained now only the question of the special gift-wrap. On the fifth floor I waited in line while the slim long box was covered in an exquisite silver paper. The bow on top was simple, as was my card, which read, "Thank you for everything. Happy Holidays". Just right.

Monday morning's session couldn't come soon enough. Careful to hide the package from my parents, I placed it inside of a brown paper bag that I crumbled and stuffed in the spiffy trashcan at the base of the elevator that would take me to the 18th floor. When I entered the consultation room, I gently placed it on Greene's desk with a soft-spoken, "Merry Christmas." But before I could get the words out of my mouth, I saw my analyst reach for the package, thrusting it towards me. "Oh, no, no. Thank you, but we cannot accept gifts from our patients. No, no, that would be counter-productive. It would interfere with the analytic process."

Tears were already welling in the corners of my eyes. Tears of humiliation and disappointment. Surely he could make an exception this one time. Surely if he saw the special socks he would relent, Freud or no Freud.

I pleaded. "Can't you just open the package? Won't you please just look at what's inside?"

"No, No, I'm sorry, Dee. Thank you very much, but just return it. Now it's time for you to lie down on the couch."

It was all I could do to restrain myself from ripping the paper off the box and thrusting its contents into his face. His expression told me the subject was closed. Stopping first to brush an imaginary speck from the little paper-covered pillow, I lay down my head and began to recount my dream.

Fifty minutes later I still talking as the session came to a close.

ßECOMING A GROWN-UP

LIFE IN CHICAGO WAS becoming more interesting. With the help of Dr. Greene, I began to take advantage of some of the activities the "Second City" had to offer. My interest in Progressive Politics pointed me to meetings and social events that Aunt Flo and Uncle Eddie had immersed themselves in several years before. Happily, I was able to combine this with my passion for acting when I discovered an agit-prop theatrical troupe called *Stage for Action*—an offshoot of the well-known New York Company, *The Worker's Laboratory Theatre*. I was quickly accepted as an actress. The group traveled from event to event, sometimes playing outdoors, spreading messages of racial equality and the importance of labor unions. I was in my element, even though, as usual, I was passed over for any ingénue role or any with a hint of glamour. One popular play was entitled "The Gentleman and the Goats." I was one in a chorus of goats, my dialogue consisting mainly of "Baaa, Baaa, Baaa." My beautiful friend Bunny, who had just been crowned AFTRA Queen of the Midwest, of course played the Gentleman's wife. It didn't matter. I was thrilled to be a part of the group. The role of the Gentleman was performed by a well-known artist of the day—Win Stracke. Stracke wrote many of the popular left-wing folk songs and was blessed with a magnificent bass voice. His close friend was Studs Terkel, who even then was acquiring a reputation as an actor/writer who spoke for the working class of Chicago. Together and individually, they often performed on Chicago radio, and because of them I managed to book several local commercials and even a bit part or two on a soap opera, thus enabling me to become a union member myself. It was known as AFTRA (American Federation of Television & Radio Artists.) I even auditioned for a brief run of "Julius Ceasar" at the University of Chicago and was awarded the role of Calpurnia. Playing the plum role of Brutas was a terrific young character actor by the name of Edward Asner. It was an exciting time in Chicago, yet I was restless. I was still living at home, still pining for Jay, and wondering if "Mr. Right" were ever to appear. Dr. Greene was encouraging — certain that my activities would point me in that direction.

With the Famous Violinist now out of my life, with Jay married, I was free to pursue other relationships. They seemed to be few and far between and usually what I termed "inappropriate" —too broke, too dull, too insecure, too unattractive. As I rejected one after another, Dr. Greene began to lose patience. "What are you going to find wrong with this one?" I complained to him that it seemed unfair that one of the young women I had met at a meeting had not one, but two serious relationships. "Bernice is nice. She's a social worker and she's very bright, but she's pretty fat. Her figure isn't nearly as good as mine. I'm sure these guys can't be very good looking," I consoled myself. But I was wrong.

I went to a party at a grand old craftsman house in the Hyde Park neighborhood. I was to meet Bernice there, knowing that both of her boyfriends were also coming. I'd get a real-live look at last. The party was in full swing, A guitar strummed to the lyrics of "It's Better With a Union Maid." We stood drinking wine together under a staircase. She pointed. "There's Jake—over there talking to that Black guy." A cute redhead, Jake was a doll. He reminded me of my old boyfriend, Stan. Bernice told me she had reached a decision. She was nearing thirty and anxious to start a family and felt she could love Jake and they would have a good future together. She intended to break up with Karl. Now I became more curious than ever about this Karl. Surely he must be less attractive than Jake or she wouldn't be so willing to throw him over. I began to wonder if he'd show.

Karl dashed though the front door as the party was winding down. There was a threat of rain in the air. He was wearing a classic tan trench coat and a brown felt hat was *squished* down over his forehead. He was the best-looking guy I had seen since the night in St. Louis that I spotted Jay leaning against his Ford station wagon. I already knew that he was just finishing Med School. Bernice is dumping this guy? Hard to believe. After the introductions were made we bantered a little before he had to leave to study for finals. The very next day, Bernice called to tell me that he had asked her for my phone number, and was it O.K. to give it to him? O.K.? O.K.? She had to be kidding!

"I hope you like jazz" he said, slamming the door of his second-hand Willys. He took my fingers as he drummed on the table in time to the notes of Bill Reinhart's sexy trumpet. We were at *The Blue Note*, the most popular Dixieland Bar on Rush Street. A perfect first date!

Three months later, Karl and I walked down the aisle at the Windermere East Hotel in Hyde Park. Graduation was near and Karl had committed to beginning an internship at Kings County Hospital in Brooklyn. He wanted me to leave with him right away. Our honeymoon would be the drive from the Midwest to New York. As a wedding gift my father had offered to replace the ailing Willys with a brand new Chevrolet—one of the first to roll off the assembly line after World War II. I would leave Chicago without a backward glance.

My beaming mother was upset only because I had insisted on a very small wedding, thus robbing her of the pleasure of gloating to her lady-friends. But it gave her no small amount of satisfaction to be able to print "Doctor" on the wedding announcements. It also enabled Bernard Greene, M.D. to file my case in the folder marked "Cured."

CHICKEN DINNER

ALL THROUGH THE 1950's I was dedicated to being both a mother to my toddlers and helpmate to my recently anointed M.D. husband. We had decided on a future in Southern California, and the San Fernando Valley was touted as a good place to start. Being a good doctor's wife in those days meant getting heavily involved in the social lives of couples with similar demographics. Most of the husbands were also just starting out in private practice. Of paramount importance was the necessity of patient referrals from colleagues. This and only this would enable us to pay our mortgages and look forward to even bigger ones in the future. The result was a series of Saturday night dinner parties. It mattered not that most of us had little in common other than the fates having thrown us together at the same time, same place. Our lack of real connection could be overcome after the first or second Manhattan— our drink of choice. Because there are a limited number of Saturdays in any given calendar, we were often booked for months in advance. Once invitations had been issued and accepted, there was little opportunity for flexibility. The Saturday night dinner party became a ritual immovable as a concert booking in Carnegie Hall.

It was our turn to host a dinner for twelve at our tract house in Van Nuys. But there was a slight glitch. My aunt Flo and Uncle Eddie were scheduled for a brief visit on that very night. Flo wouldn't hear of my canceling, in fact, she insisted that she and Eddie join in the fun. This group was a far cry from their bunch of liberal pals in Chicago and I had more than a few trepidations. Not to worry, Flo insisted, she'd play the role of visiting aunt to the hilt, besides helping me to serve and clean up.

By the time Flo and Eddie arrived early Saturday, dinner was planned and prepared. We young wives had already begun the pattern of trying to outdo one another regarding the menu. (Later we would leave that to professional caterers.)

With me, it was a question of making something very, very easy that looked very, very difficult. I was already an expert in the art of the short cut, having discovered a marvelous barbecue sauce that was sold only at Love's, a restaurant on Ventura Blvd. If I was careful to dispose of the container, no one need ever know that I had not slaved over the sauce from scratch. Freshly cut up chicken was laid out in a roasting pan, then covered and basted with this mouth-watering stuff before being popped into the 325- degree oven. Accompanying dish was instant brown rice with almonds, and *voila!* A tempting, sure-fire, gourmet dinner.

Flo came into the kitchen to inspect. "This is it? This all you're serving? Don't they have a choice? What if they don't like chicken?"

"Don't be silly, everybody likes chicken!" I cried out with pre-vegan assurance.

My DNA was similar to Flo's in many respects, but her passion for *more not less* was where it parted company, my mother's genes kicking in. *Just enough to go around* was my Mom's motto, whereas Flo's could best be summed up as *the more the merrier, the bigger the better.*

Never in all her years of entertaining for hordes of family and friends had Flo seen such a Spartan array of party food. I had allocated one medium piece of chicken for each guest, plus just a few extra for those pigs who might want seconds. That would be plenty. The chicken had been purchased from Phil's, the very best fresh poultry store in the Valley. Money was still tight, there was no need to overdo. Why clutter the refrigerator with leftovers? Of course, Flo and Eddie had unexpectedly arrived to eat with us, which cut down the number of extra pieces somewhat. Little did I worry, as I intended to serve plenty of onion cheese dip and chopped liver with the cocktails.

The little party was going off well. By the time we moved to the dining area at the far end of the living room everyone was in a good mood. And ravenous. With Flo's help, I began filling plates in the kitchen. One healthy piece of chicken accompanied by a good-sized portion of brown rice. A salad and other side dishes were already on the table.

The chicken with the secret sauce was delicious— a huge hit. One by one, guests requested seconds. Flo and I went back and forth to the kitchen for refills. As the roasting pan emptied, a certain amount of panic set in. I glared at Karl when he, too, requested a second. Behind the closed door of the kitchen, Flo and I exchanged silent prayers that the remaining thighs and breasts would hold out. There was really no backup plan. Once they were gone, that was it. There would be no referrals for my husband out of this dinner party! Finally everyone seemed sated and we were down to one drumstick. I walked through the swinging door and took my place at the foot of the table where I scooped up a few mouthfuls of the brown rice. The Manhattans had sustained me. Relieved that the crisis was over I could begin to enjoy myself. But at that moment, my darling aunt sashayed brazenly out of the kitchen, carrying a platter heaped with rice and sauce and topped by one chicken drumstick. "Would anyone care for more?" she asked cheerfully, "there's plenty in the kitchen!" No one did. I could have murdered her.

When the door had shut on the last of the guests and Flo and I began KP duty, we began to laugh. We laughed almost at hard as Flo and her sister Lily had laughed at Flo's rotund blind date many years before. And I laughed with the relief of knowing that once again, as with the flower petals at Flo's wedding, I had somehow managed to come out even. "There's more in the kitchen," I mocked. Flo was nonplused. "There *was* more," she insisted, "a lot more. I just never said more of what."

BETTY AND JUNE

AUNT FLO ALWAYS CALLED it my Green Eyed Monster. I had suffered from a severe case of envy since I was a little girl, but I hoped that marriage to a doctor, the birth of two perfect babies plus a house in the suburbs would suffice to quell it. Now, as I eyed the attractive woman reclining on a chaise lounge, I knew that enough would never be enough. Here was someone who obviously had everything. Her name was June, otherwise known as Mrs. George Wayne.

It was 1960 and I had completed my Freudian psychoanalysis some ten years earlier. In his wood-paneled office on North Michigan Blvd. in Chicago, Dr. Greene had cheerfully dismissed me as I prepared to wend my way to the West Coast with my new husband. The fact that I was leaving my family over two thousand miles behind was considered a big plus. "Chicago is toxic for you. Go with a clean slate, forget about your transference to me, focus on your husband. Now you will be able to be a help-mate to him, to bask in his new career, to easily achieve orgasm."

A smile crossed his face as he blessed me with a hug on my shoulders, certain that my analysis was a total success. Mission accomplished.

But if my analysis was so complete, why was the monster still on my back? Why was there a nagging feeling as I watched the silver-haired George Wayne joyfully shaking hands as he accepted praise for his new venture?

Prior to this time, mentally ill patients requiring hospitalization in the Los Angeles area had a choice of only a few large, impersonal institutions. It took much financial backing and a lot of *chutzpah* to become the first M.D. to buck the trend. My husband Karl had only recently received his credentials to practice psychotherapy, a newly recognized specialty. The race for private patients was on, and it was tough. The medical clique in the San Fernando Valley, where we had settled, was already firmly established. Since the AMA forbid any advertising or publicity, referrals from other doctors was the main pathway to success and solvency. Socializing was hardly Karl's forte, which accounted for his enthusiasm at the prospect of working in a bona-fide psychiatric setting without having to host what we termed "lavish doctor dinner parties."

Dr. Wayne named his hospital *Edgemont Sanitarium* because of its street address. Just before its official opening, he hosted a gala open house for members of the medical community. I was thrilled to attend. The occasion called for the purchase of a bright yellow flowered dress and a pair of high-heeled white pumps. The facility was on large spacious grounds in a lovely old section of Los Angeles. Guides were assigned small groups to tour the hospital. Not certain what to expect, I was totally unprepared for what I saw. Just over the threshold, in the reception area, hung a large watercolor showing a long hilly country road with a small house perched on top in the distance. An isolated figure is ascending that road, determined to make it up to the house. Mesmerized, I stared at this work until our young guide coaxed me inside me to catch up with his group. Wide corridors opened to a series of private rooms, all tastefully decorated in pastel colors. No snake pit here. No bars on the windows or other telltale signs of what was known as a "closed ward." What was most surprising was the impressive artwork. Above each bed hung an original painting, each different, every one outstanding. Not a white-faced clown or a bouquet of daisies to be found. Decorating the wide hallways were several black and white lithographs, provocative, enigmatic, yet never disturbing. We rounded a corner to discover the walls covered with a series of colorful collages. Was this a hospital or an art gallery? I brazenly sauntered away from the group for a closer inspection. My hand reached up to touch a piece of fabric to see if it was real or painted. Like a museum guard, my guide quickly reprimanded me. "Sorry. I just had to see if this was fabric or paint. I m so impressed with all these paintings!"

"Would you care to meet the artist?"

"Artist? You mean one man did all of these?"

"Not a man, a woman. Dr. Wayne's wife, June."

Outside on a terrace, cocktails were being served. An unassuming lovely woman relaxed on a chaise lounge, inhaling a cigarette. My guide introduced us, then left me to gush, "Mrs. Wayne, I can't believe all the art work inside is yours!"

"Call me June. And why is that? Why can't you believe that I am the artist?"

I stammered. "Well, it's just that…that the work is so…so powerful. So varied. I had no idea that Dr. Wayne's wife was so gifted." I was rewarded for this naive statement with a slight smile and a perfunctory, "Thank you." And then, June Wayne pointed to a chair at her side. "Sit. Tell me something about yourself."

Throngs of people were milling about, many of whom wished to speak to her, but for the next half-hour June Wayne's attention was focused on me. Sensing her genuine interest, my shyness was overcome by my need to connect. After giving her my vital statistics, I began pouring out my frustrations with my recent move from the East coast and my present life as suburban mother of two and wife of a struggling young physician. The bright yellow dress belied the misery I felt inside. "You couldn't know what it is like. You have a husband who is so charming, so successful, who created this marvelous facility. You have it all."

"You think so? You really think I have it all because I am Mrs. Doctor Wayne? You imagine I am basking in reflected glory?"

"Well, no, not exactly. It's just that you must be so proud of him and of this place. Helping to create it..."

"Let me tell you. It's true, I selected the colors for the walls of this edifice. It's true my artwork is hanging in the halls, but this is George's creation, his profession. I have nothing further to contribute."

What precisely did she mean? Didn't she realize how much she could aid her husband's career by being a hostess, and by making him proud of her through her art?

I glanced up to see Dr. Wayne flashing his seductive white smile and handshaking vigorously. Then I located my own Karl sitting quietly to one side, morosely drawing on his pipe, detached as usual, reluctant to circulate. Was this any way to ingratiate himself? Was this the way to get referrals? Sure, I wanted to be his helpmate but it required a little effort on his part. June Wayne went on speaking.

"Believe me, you don't really want to live your life through another person. You've already told me about your love of acting. What's holding you back? Why are you just quietly becoming a full-time wife and mother? You've already discovered that's not going to be fulfilling enough for you."

If ever I were to have an epiphany, this was the moment. As I absorbed these words, I saw George Wayne eyeing a svelte, sexy blonde who appeared at his side. A moment later, he took her arm and led her inside. June glanced quickly in their direction, then turned her attention back to me. An entire scenario became clear in a flash: George Wayne might have been a leader in his field, but he was just a man, after all.

"Tell me, have you ever heard of a woman called Betty Friedan?" June asked. The name had a vaguely familiar ring. "I assure you, you will. Remember that name."

A short time later, Friedan's "Feminine Mystic" was published. *It is easier to live through someone else than to become complete yourself,* she wrote, and then went on to assure us: *A woman has got to be able to say, and not feel guilty, who am I, and what do I want out of life?*

Long before Aunt Flo sent me the book as a gift, I had been given the message loud and clear from June Wayne. She relinquished her title of Mrs. Doctor, secured a grant from the Ford Foundation, and established "The Tamarind Institute," where she revived the long neglected art of lithography printing. Her accomplishments were legion: A PBS tribute to her successful mother entitled, "The Dorothy Stories" was followed by many outstanding shows at major galleries. She scarcely seemed to notice when George Wayne went on to marry his Hungarian Trophy Wife, for she had already reached her house at the top of the hill.

As for me, most nights around 7 p.m. I could be found backstage at a Little Theatre in the San Fernando Valley hurriedly applying grease paint in time for my entrance. Noise and laughter erupted around me as actors gossiped and ran lines. No one seemed bothered by the unmistaken odor of lamb chop grease coming from my hands, nor the bits of macaroni and cheese clinging to my fingers. The hill was still steep, but I no longer felt alone as I climbed it.